"This book takes you on a ~
genetics, free will, positive ps~
within an evangelical Christian framework. Fascinated, I read this in
one sitting. It is a wonderful, summative, yet critical introduction to
thinking Christianly about psychology."

Everett L. Worthington Jr., author, *Moving Forward: Six Steps to Forgiving Yourself and Breaking Free from the Past*

"An insightful account of contemporary psychology and its relation to the Christian faith. Jones helps readers understand where psychology is today and how it got there. He shows how Christians can learn from and contribute to psychology while preserving a critical perspective rooted in biblical faith. A wise and helpful book."

C. Stephen Evans, Professor of Philosophy and Humanities, Baylor University; author, *God and Moral Obligation*

"This insightful, incisive critique of contemporary psychology is only possible because Dr. Jones is so deeply knowledgeable about both Christianity and psychology. As always, his writing is clear, direct, and thought provoking. Reading this book is like taking a guided tour of contemporary issues in psychology, led by one of the finest Christian thinkers of our time."

Mark R. McMinn, Professor of Psychology, George Fox University; author, *Psychology, Theology, and Spirituality in Christian Counseling*

"Jones has written a concise yet substantial Christian perspective and critique of the field of psychology, focusing on the key areas of neuroscience, behavior genetics, positive psychology, and the psychology of religion. I highly recommend this very helpful book as essential reading for beginning students in psychology."

Siang-Yang Tan, Professor of Psychology, Fuller Theological Seminary; author, *Counseling and Psychotherapy: A Christian Perspective*

PSYCHOLOGY

RECLAIMING THE
CHRISTIAN INTELLECTUAL TRADITION

David S. Dockery, series editor

CONSULTING EDITORS

Hunter Baker

Timothy George

Niel Nielson

Philip G. Ryken

Michael J. Wilkins

John D. Woodbridge

OTHER RCIT VOLUMES:

The Great Tradition of Christian Thinking, David S. Dockery and
Timothy George

The Liberal Arts, Gene C. Fant Jr.

Political Thought, Hunter Baker

Literature, Louis Markos

Philosophy, David K. Naugle

Christian Worldview, Philip G. Ryken

Art and Music, Paul Munson and Joshua Farris Drake

PSYCHOLOGY
A STUDENT'S GUIDE

Stanton L. Jones

::: CROSSWAY

WHEATON, ILLINOIS

Psychology: A Student's Guide

Copyright © 2014 by Stanton L. Jones

Published by Crossway
    1300 Crescent Street
    Wheaton, Illinois 60187

Cover design: Jon McGrath, Simplicated Studio

First printing 2014

Printed in the United States of America

Scripture quotations are from the ESV® Bible (*The Holy Bible, English Standard Version*®), copyright © 2001 by Crossway. 2011 Text Edition. Used by permission. All rights reserved.

Trade paperback ISBN: 978-1-4335-3978-7
ePub ISBN: 978-1-4335-3981-7
PDF ISBN: 978-1-4335-3979-4
Mobipocket ISBN: 978-1-4335-3980-0

Library of Congress Cataloging-in-Publication Data

Jones, Stanton L.
    Psychology : a student's guide / Stanton L. Jones.
      pages cm. — (Reclaiming the Christian intellectual tradition)
    Includes bibliographical references and index.
    ISBN 978-1-4335-3978-7 (tp)
    1. Christianity—Psychology—Textbooks. 2. Psychology and religion—Textbooks. 3. Psychology—Philosophy—Textbooks.
I. Title.
BR110.J585   2014
261.5'15--dc23   2014020704

Crossway is a publishing ministry of Good News Publishers.

VP		24	23	22	21	20	19	18	17	16	15	14
15	14	13	12	11	10	9	8	7	6	5	4	3	2	1

To Emily, Canon, Brady, Aaron, and Brian; five wonderful people whose addition to our family—by marriage as our new children or by birth as our grandchildren—has expanded the scope of our joy and our experience of love. Thank you.

CONTENTS

SERIES PREFACE

RECLAIMING THE CHRISTIAN INTELLECTUAL TRADITION

The Reclaiming the Christian Intellectual Tradition series is designed to provide an overview of the distinctive way the church has read the Bible, formulated doctrine, provided education, and engaged the culture. The contributors to this series all agree that personal faith and genuine Christian piety are essential for the life of Christ followers and for the church. These contributors also believe that helping others recognize the importance of serious thinking about God, Scripture, and the world needs a renewed emphasis at this time in order that the truth claims of the Christian faith can be passed along from one generation to the next. The study guides in this series will enable us to see afresh how the Christian faith shapes how we live, how we think, how we write books, how we govern society, and how we relate to one another in our churches and social structures. The richness of the Christian intellectual tradition provides guidance for the complex challenges that believers face in this world.

This series is particularly designed for Christian students and others associated with college and university campuses, including faculty, staff, trustees, and other various constituents. The contributors to the series will explore how the Bible has been interpreted in the history of the church, as well as how theology has been formulated. They will ask: How does the Christian faith influence our understanding of culture, literature, philosophy, government, beauty, art, or work? How does the Christian intellectual tradition help us understand truth? How does the Christian intellectual tradition shape our approach to education? We believe that this series is not only timely but that it meets an important need, because the secular culture in which we now find ourselves is, at best, indifferent to the Christian faith, and the Christian world—at least in its more popular forms—tends to be confused about the beliefs, heritage, and tradition associated with the Christian faith.

At the heart of this work is the challenge to prepare a generation of Christians to think Christianly, to engage the academy and the culture, and to serve church and society. We believe that both the breadth and the depth of the Christian intellectual tradition need to be reclaimed, revitalized, renewed, and revived for us to carry forward this work. These study guides will seek to provide a framework to help introduce students to the great tradition of Christian thinking, seeking to highlight its importance for understanding the world, its significance for serving both church and society, and its application for Christian thinking and learning. The series is a starting point for exploring important ideas and issues such as truth, meaning, beauty, and justice.

We trust that the series will help introduce readers to the apostles, church fathers, Reformers, philosophers, theologians, historians, and a wide variety of other significant thinkers. In addition to well-known leaders such as Clement, Origen, Augustine, Thomas Aquinas, Martin Luther, and Jonathan Edwards, readers will be pointed to William Wilberforce, G. K. Chesterton, T. S. Eliot, Dorothy Sayers, C. S. Lewis, Johann Sebastian Bach, Isaac Newton, Johannes Kepler, George Washington Carver, Elizabeth Fox-Genovese, Michael Polanyi, Henry Luke Orombi, and many others. In doing so, we hope to introduce those who throughout history have demonstrated that it is indeed possible to be serious about the life of the mind while simultaneously being deeply committed Christians. These efforts to strengthen serious Christian thinking and scholarship will not be limited to the study of theology, scriptural interpretation, or philosophy, even though these areas provide the framework for understanding the Christian faith for all other areas of exploration. In order for us to reclaim and advance the Christian intellectual tradition, we must have some understanding of the tradition itself. The volumes in this series seek to explore this tradition and its application for our twenty-first-century world. Each volume contains a glossary, study questions, and a list of resources for further study, which we trust will provide helpful guidance for our readers.

I am deeply grateful to the series editorial committee: Timothy George, John Woodbridge, Michael Wilkins, Niel Nielson, Philip Ryken, and Hunter Baker. Each of these colleagues joins me in thanking our various contributors for their fine work. We all express our appreciation to Justin Taylor, Jill Carter, Allan Fisher, Lane Dennis, and the Crossway team for their enthusiastic support for the project. We offer the project with the hope that students will be helped, faculty and Christian leaders will be encouraged, institutions will be strengthened, churches will be built up, and, ultimately, that God will be glorified.

Soli Deo Gloria
David S. Dockery
Series Editor

ACKNOWLEDGMENTS

I am especially indebted to Ray Phinney, William Struthers, and Philip Ryken, with whom I discussed various ideas for this volume; Jay Wood, who helped me with some philosophical concepts and resources; Cynthia Neal Kimball and Richard Butman, who read specific chapters and offered extremely wise suggestions and criticisms (some of which I chose to ignore—sorry); and especially to Sarah Miglio, whose careful reading of the entire manuscript, editorial suggestions, encouragement, and thoughtfulness came at the right moment. Thanks to Magnolia Laya and Dianne McCarty for structuring my professional life and creating space on the margins for this project to come to fruition; you two are amazing.

I acknowledge with gratitude the wonderful Christian intellectual community of Wheaton College, from which I continually draw spiritual and intellectual inspiration.

Finally, my deepest gratitude goes to my ever-supportive and patient soul mate, Brenna, without whose strength, depth, and forgiveness my life would be infinitely diminished.

INTRODUCTION

In the Bible, the prophets and apostles ask various forms of the question, What is a human being? (e.g., Job 7:17; 15:14; Ps. 144:3; Heb. 2:6). "Who are we? What are we? What are we supposed to be doing? Who are we in relation to everything else?"[1] They do not leave the question unanswered but give concise, general answers describing human beings as created in God's image and in relationship to the one true God. Do we need more than that?

You have picked up this book because you are interested in the field of psychology and seek a general understanding of *how Christians should approach this field*. I commend you for this interest but warn you that the answers are complex, first because the contemporary discipline of psychology has been conceptualized and pursued from a fundamental commitment to turning *away* from answers from theology and religious traditions in favor of the findings from supposedly objective, neutral scientific methods. As we shall see, careful thought and contemporary scholarship challenge the supposed objectivity and neutrality of this approach (chapter 1). Further, many psychologists manifest disinterest or even antagonism toward religion, especially toward institutionalized, traditional religious faith (i.e., Christianity; see chapter 6); these attitudes show in their work.

The answers are also complex because, while careful biblical study gives us many rich perspectives on human existence, human growth, and ministry to those in distress, the guidance offered is often more skeletal and abstract than we might want. For instance, you'll discover in chapter 2 that the most fundamental truth about

---

[1] Marc Cortez, *Embodied Souls, Ensouled Bodies: An Exercise in Christological Anthropology and Its Significance for the Mind/Body Debate* (New York: T & T Clark, 2008), 1.

human existence—that we are made in the very image of God—has been the subject of theological dispute since the earliest days of the church. This truth is *simultaneously* fundamental and indispensable but also terribly complex and vague.

Finally, the answers are complex because psychology is so diverse. The discipline spans from neuroscientific studies of single neurons in simple organisms on the one hand, to the measurement of cultural attitudes about religion and their impact upon individuals, families, and organizations. The applied facets of the discipline range from studies of animal learning to behavior modification of the profoundly developmentally disabled, to problem-oriented psychotherapy with individuals and groups, to organizational and social interventions to foster enhanced functioning. Such complexity befuddles the formulation of any simple understanding of how faith and psychology relate.

The field of psychology should be approached by Christians with enthusiasm for all it offers from the vast cornucopia of research probing the nature of human existence. At the same time, the field of psychology should be approached by the Christian with caution because much of the field needs to be reinterpreted or challenged on the basis of fundamental Christian convictions. We should approach psychology *critically*, teasing out aspects incompatible with Christian faith, challenging key concepts and rethinking them on the basis of scriptural truth. But we also should approach psychology *constructively*, seeking to make positive use of its best theory and research and striving to synthesize this into a system congruent with Christian conviction to advance the scientific quest.

It is this two-part dynamic of critical and constructive Christian engagement with the field that I regard as the "integration of psychology and Christian faith."[2] I will expand on this definition

---

[2] Stanton L. Jones, "A Constructive Relationship for Religion with the Science and Profession of Psychology: Perhaps the Boldest Model Yet," *American Psychologist* 49 (1994): 184–99; Stanton L. Jones and Richard Butman, *Modern Psychotherapies: A Comprehensive Christian Appraisal*, 2nd ed. (Downers Grove, IL: InterVarsity, 2011); Stanton Jones, "An Integration View," in *Psychology and Christianity: Five Views*, 2nd ed., ed. Eric L. Johnson (Downers Grove, IL: InterVarsity, 2010), 101–28.

of *integration* in the second chapter. It is my hope to model such Christian engagement in this brief work. But first, in chapter 1 I place psychology in context of the great intellectual tradition of the West. Psychology's fit within this intellectual history can be hard to discern for the student new to the field, in part because of psychology's pervasive penetration into popular culture: psychological thinking seems almost second nature; it is in the air we breathe and the water we drink. In chapter 2 I outline the fundamentals of biblical perspectives on human beings and elaborate a bit on the task of the integration of psychology and Christianity.

Because a review of and response to the entire field of psychology would be quite impossible in a brief book such as this, I present to the reader four case studies from representative facets of the field. Together, these allow us to engage some of the most challenging and fundamental questions about how Christian faith relates to the field, hopefully equipping us with a basic understanding of how to responsibly engage psychology as thoughtful Christians.

1

PSYCHOLOGY IN ITS INTELLECTUAL CONTEXT

Some who trace the history of the field of psychology suggest that the discipline leapt into existence in Europe as a scientific splinter from the field of philosophy initiated by professor of philosophy Wilhelm Wundt. Wundt—as the story goes—put aside the increasingly fruitless speculations of philosophy about the human person and decided instead to do what scientists must do: build a foundation of sure knowledge by focusing on "the data."

SCIENCE, PSYCHOLOGY, AND THEOLOGICAL REFLECTION UNITED

In reality, psychology did not simply leap into existence in the late nineteenth century. Psychology, as more thorough histories document,[1] has been around in some form since the dawn of human self-reflection and intellectual inquiry. Our understandings of the human condition as well as of the world around us have always drawn upon "data" of some sort, with that data interpreted through human reason operating in the context of a set of presumed understandings that have shaped and guided that inquiry.

Here, I want to pay particular attention to the "presumed understandings that have shaped and guided" inquiry. Specifically, I want to outline how psychology has developed in the context of Christian reflection and more recently in a Western intellectual

---

[1] E.g., Daniel Robinson, *An Intellectual History of Psychology*, rev. ed. (New York: Macmillan, 1976).

tradition in which Christian and other religious perspectives have been pushed aside.

The most rigorous ancient outlines of human psychology are attributable to Plato, Aristotle, and other great ancient Greek thinkers, who explored human motivation and reason, the purposes and shape of human community, the form of optimal character, and the nature of human dysfunctions. Concurrent with but independent from the development of Greek thought, the Hebrews developed their own religious and intellectual traditions in the context of a dizzying array of ancient Near Eastern cultures, resulting—by the inspiration of the Holy Spirit and the self-revelation of God the Father—in the Old Testament.

While the Old Testament contains little that looks like psychology by today's standards, it is nevertheless true that there is much "psychological" material there, particularly fundamental understandings of the nature of what it means to be a human being. The Old Testament depicts the first human beings—despite being "very good" (Gen. 1:31)—as succumbing to sin and reaping the full consequences for themselves and all their ancestors. Old Testament passages speak of emotions, motivations, beliefs, character and virtue, social institutions, and many facets of the human condition. Wisdom Literature such as Proverbs offers concrete guidance for proper human development, for parenting, for the development of moral character, for shaping social relationships, and other topics. The moral laws of Exodus and Deuteronomy provide a backdrop of God's intent for human action that help us understand what it means to be human. While this may fall short of constituting an academic discipline, the Old Testament does offer rich teaching about what it means to be a human being.

The first book in this study guide series explores the rise and evolution of the Christian intellectual movement.[2] Grounded in

---

[2] David Dockery and Timothy George, *The Great Tradition of Christian Thinking: A Student's Guide*, Reclaiming the Christian Intellectual Tradition (Wheaton, IL: Crossway, 2012).

God's truth as revealed in the Old Testament, the expanding early church first received a new set of God's revelations from the earthly ministry of the Lord Jesus Christ and then further instruction from the inspired writings of the apostles—the New Testament. Then as the church grew explosively throughout the Roman world and other areas, problems arose in key theological areas.

Many of the growing number of Gentile converts were blessed with thorough preparation in the great intellectual traditions of the Greco-Roman world and used this intellectual preparation in service of Christ. The early Christian church did *not* take a stance of rejection toward secular knowledge but rather sought to purify and properly use secular thought in service of Christ. Early Christian thinkers used the work of Plato, Aristotle, and others as tools in their theological and practical endeavors, with these resources interpreted in light of the teachings of the Scriptures. Dockery and George note that the "third century saw the rise of schools, intertwined with classical learning, science, philosophy, and centers of art. The Christian intellectual tradition shaped by serious biblical interpretation began to develop and mature in the Schools of Alexandria [Egypt] and Antioch."[3]

Thus began the great Christian intellectual tradition, including science more broadly and specifically Christian psychological inquiry. Sophisticated forms of psychological thought emerged in the early church as pastors, bishops, theologians, and others struggled to understand how to best guide the formation of Christian character, heal the wounds of the broken and struggling among their flocks, and offer the best pastoral guidance in all circumstances. Augustine (fifth century) developed sophisticated reflections on human psychology grounded in the Scriptures and "flavored by the philosophical tradition inspired by Plato."[4] Pope Gregory the Great (sixth century) developed a sophisticated pastoral psychology con-

---

[3] Ibid., 31.
[4] Eric L. Johnson, "A Brief History of Christians in Psychology," *Psychology and Christianity: Five Views*, 2nd ed., ed. Eric L. Johnson (Downers Grove, IL: InterVarsity, 2010), 12.

taining a kind of personality theory that was to guide pastoral care in the Western church for centuries to come.[5]

The difficult period between the decline of the Roman Empire and the rise of the European Renaissance has long been labeled as the "Dark Ages" by secular chroniclers of intellectual history, some of whom claim that the Christian tradition suppressed the advance of scientific/secular knowledge until progress reemerged in the Renaissance as a result of the rediscovery in the West of the work of Aristotle. Many historians now dispute this interpretation as wrong on at least three fronts.

First, it is clear that much intellectual work worthy of respect was going on during this period. Second, the collapse of the Roman Empire and the cultural turmoil that ensued made profound intellectual progress challenging; that the medieval Church succeeded in preserving much of ancient human knowledge was quite remarkable. Third, the characterization of the Renaissance as an intellectual step forward is exaggerated. Much of Renaissance thought was intertwined with magic, spiritism, superstition, alchemy, and ignorance. For instance, astrology reemerged and flourished during the Renaissance because Aristotelian cosmology made astrology a respectable part of *natural* science; this cosmology assumed that the celestial spheres exerted influences on daily life through "the *natural* forces that link heaven and earth."[6]

Still, it is true that there were gaps in intellectual progress during the Dark Ages compared to the advances of the Scientific Revolution that followed. One fundamental problem of the period was the reliance of the Catholic Church (until the thirteenth century) on a synthesis of Christian theology with Platonic philosophy. There were limitations to the kinds of intellectual progress that could be made based on Platonic thought, which helps to

---

[5] Thomas Oden, *Care of Souls in the Classic Tradition* (Philadelphia: Fortress, 1984).
[6] David Lindberg, *The Beginnings of Western Science: The European Scientific Tradition in Philosophical, Religious, and Institutional Context, 600 B.C. to A.D. 1450* (Chicago: University of Chicago Press, 1992), 102, emphasis original.

explain the explosive impact of what transpired in the thirteenth century.

THE FOUNDATIONS OF THE SCIENTIFIC REVOLUTION

The writings of Aristotle had been lost in the European West but were well preserved and utilized in the expanding Islamic world. In the twelfth and thirteenth centuries, Christian, Jewish, and Islamic scholars in Spain collaborated in exploring Aristotle's thought, resulting in challenges to Platonic thought. A new synthesis of Christian theology with the thought of Aristotle began to emerge, particularly in Paris. Thomas Aquinas, perhaps one of the most brilliant intellects ever, used the thought of Aristotle to forge new reflections in theology, philosophy, and all of human knowledge, including insight on the nature of human psychology, and their applications to pastoral care. The resulting synthesis is often called Thomistic or Scholastic philosophy and theology.

It is common to attribute the foundations of modern science to Aristotle's renewed influence in the thirteenth century, but this is simplistic and misguided. In contrast to the sweeping deductions of Plato, Aristotle did use induction, reasoning from bits of "data" upward toward generalizations. But there is no such thing as pure induction; Aristotle's philosophical approach to the physical cosmos and psychology built on many a priori assumptions, including many that were false. Aquinas was cautious in his use of Aristotle, but for several generations after, Aquinas's disciples were aggressive and undiscerning in their embrace of Aristotle.

And then something happened that set important foundations for the Scientific Revolution. Because of the excessive promotion of the philosophy of Aristotle over Christian theology by some of the intellectual descendants of Aquinas, others arose within the pre-Reformation church and began to challenge these assumptions. For example, the bishop of Paris issued a series of *condemnations* of such views. For instance, Aristotle had proposed that it was impossible for a void, a true vacuum, to exist. By Aristotle's pre-Christian understanding, even a god could not make a vacuum; it was simply impossible. Some Christian thinkers followed Aristotle and argued that God could not make a void; God's power was limited by Aristotle's presumed *necessary truths*.

"Aristotle had attempted to describe the world not simply as it is, but as it must be. In 1277 [the bishop of Paris] declared, in opposition to Aristotle, that the world is whatever its omnipotent Creator chose to make it."[7] The significance of this cannot be understated. Such an assertion of *contingency* serves to limit assertions that the physical world, or human character, *must* be a certain way because of the dictates of human reason.[8] Rather, the mind-set that emerges is that things could be constituted any number of ways by God's contingent and free will, and thus we actually need to investigate physical (or human) reality to see how things really are rather than use merely rational deduction. This mind-set is part of *an excellent foundation for the advance of science*.

In fact, a number of other Christian principles proved to be fruitful in solidifying the foundation for the developing scientific revolution of the following centuries, by (1) providing a theological and biblical foundation for seeing physical reality as good and thus worthy of study; (2) motivating the search for universal laws by understanding the physical world as the creation of a rational lawgiver who made the world to reflect his rational mind; and (3) providing personal motives for scientists, such as improving the world to bring glory to God or helping to provide rational evidence for God's existence.[9]

---

[7] Ibid., 239.
[8] As in, "The characteristics of the natural world are contingent upon the creational will of God."
[9] John H. Brooke, *Science and Religion* (Cambridge, UK: Cambridge University Press, 1991); see also Colin Russell, *Cross-Currents: Interactions Between Science and Faith* (Leicester, UK: InterVarsity, 1985).

WARFARE BETWEEN SCIENCE AND RELIGION: REAL AND IMAGINED

What we understand today as modern science began to emerge in the centuries that followed, thanks to the foundations laid by theological developments in the Catholic Church and in the emerging Protestant Reformation that began in the fifteenth century. Much of the emerging scientific inquiry and development (broadly conceived, and psychology more narrowly) was integrally intertwined with and fostered by Christian theological reflection, and many great scientists were devout Christians.

But, frankly, this was not the story I grew up hearing about the relationship between science and religion. In many places in Western culture today, religion and science are portrayed as antagonists. Many secular, anti-religious scholars have asserted that religion has always stood for dogmatic certainty, superstition, and authoritarian control, while science is on an open-minded, noble quest for truth, and thus that the two forces have been locked in conflict since the emergence of modern science. This "standard account" was systematized in the English-speaking world toward the end of the nineteenth century—at the high-water mark of the intellectual movement called the Enlightenment—by the work of two ardent proponents.

John William Draper authored the highly influential diatribe *History of the Conflict Between Religion and Science* (1874), which has stayed in print for fourteen decades. Draper claimed that the Roman Church had perpetually displayed "a bitter and mortal animosity" toward science and fostered brutal persecution of scientists and other nonconformists. Draper even claims, wrongly, that the church had declared that "all knowledge is to be found in the Scriptures" and constitutes "all that he [God] intended us to know."[10] This account suggests that the church attempted to maintain a stranglehold on thought to perpetuate its control in

---

[10] Lindberg, *Beginnings of Western Science*, 19.

society. This control began to weaken when the Renaissance inspired human inquiry unfettered by a constricting dominance by Christian theology. Then scientists like Galileo[11] and philosophers like Descartes launched an intellectual revolution, insisting on the primacy and power of rationality and the rejection of tradition and superstition. The secret to the pursuit of truth, in this understanding, was method: the scientific method guaranteed (or at the very least radically enhanced) the procurement of true knowledge. Similarly, Andrew Dickason White's *A History of the Warfare of Science with Theology in Christendom* (1896; also still in print) painted an almost identical picture of all-out warfare between science and religion.

As a result of these works and others like them, many today are prone to believe in the warfare between science and religion. For example, the prestigious National Academy of Sciences issued a terse resolution in 1981 stating, "Religion and science are separate and *mutually exclusive realms of human thought* whose presentation in the same context leads to misunderstanding of both scientific theory and religious belief."[12] Instead of scientific and theological reasoning being understood as seamlessly interwoven and mutually supportive, the Enlightenment *dis-integrated* what had previously been a seamless and mutually supportive relationship. Deep wedges were driven between Christian reflection and science in general. It is these movements and their repercussions that have created the need today for integration, the intentional bringing together of Christian reflection and secular scholarship.

But for the possibility of integration to be intellectually defensible, we need a deeper understanding of the Enlightenment.

---

[11] Galileo is often presented as the scientific antithesis to religious belief. He was, in fact, a devout Christian and had quite articulate views about the trustworthiness of Scripture and its compatibility with truth from the natural world. For a brief presentation on this, see Mark Noll, *Jesus Christ and the Life of the Mind* (Grand Rapids, MI: Eerdmans, 2011), 102–5.

[12] *Science and Creationism: A View from the National Academy of Sciences* (Washington, DC: National Academy of Sciences, 1984), emphasis added.

A DEEPER UNDERSTANDING OF
THE ENLIGHTENMENT

In Draper's and White's account, the Enlightenment established that science is a purely rational pursuit of facts, and religion is about irrationality. Stephen Toulmin criticizes this "Standard Account,"[13] suggesting a different and better narrative of the rise of the Enlightenment and the warfare account.

Toulmin suggests that the Enlightenment exploded in Europe because the continent was wracked with war for over a century. An economic depression and devastating weather conditions resulted in widespread hunger; massive unemployment created a huge pool of mercenaries to fuel constant warfare. Much of this warfare was, at least on the surface, religious in nature: Catholics against various types of Protestants, and Protestants against Protestants; neighbors killed neighbors in the name of Christianity. This insanity fueled in some intellectuals a deeply rooted conviction that *religion* was the enemy of concord and understanding. These intellectuals desired to find some foundation for human knowledge other than religion.

There was a preliminary phase of the Enlightenment, a humanist phase of the late sixteenth and early seventeenth centuries that was fundamentally Christian and manifested sincere religious devotion as typified by Montaigne, Erasmus, Rabelais, and Shakespeare. But according to Toulmin, the second and more secular phase of the Enlightenment overwhelmed the first and was typified by Descartes. The first Christian humanistic phase sought modest understanding, but the second phase reached for timeless theoretical certainty. And it was presumed that to reach such perfect truth, one had to rely upon human reason *rather than and separate from the teachings and authority of religion.*

The philosophy of René Descartes is often summed up by his

---

[13] Stephen Toulmin, *Cosmopolis: The Hidden Agenda of Modernity* (Chicago: University of Chicago Press, 1990).

famous statement, "I think, therefore I am." Descartes's method was the method of doubt, of setting aside all assumptions and religious teachings to reach for that which was indisputable and noninferential.[14] Everything could be doubted except the reality that *if* I can doubt and think, I must exist. Descartes believed he had found the absolute foundation for secure, indisputable human knowledge and from there built upwards. Other philosophers crucial to the developing Enlightenment such as John Locke and David Hume joined Descartes in *placing the knowing self, the person as an isolated, reasoning being, at the foundation of knowledge.*

It is vital to note the isolation or alienation of religious faith, belief, and truth from the task of the pursuit of knowledge. The definition of the Enlightenment by Immanuel Kant in 1784 is telling:

> *Enlightenment is the human being's emergence from his self-incurred minority.* Minority is the inability to make use of one's own understanding without direction from another. This minority *is self-incurred* when its cause lies not in lack of understanding but in lack of resolution and courage to use it without direction from another. *Sapere aude!* (dare to be wise!) Have courage to make use of your *own* understanding! is thus the motto of enlightenment.[15]

From under whose direction, tutelage, or oversight does the enlightened individual need to emerge? For most Enlightenment thinkers, it was religious doctrine and authority. Repudiation of religious authority in favor of the unencumbered *reason of the individual* was integral to the Enlightenment project.

If the individual was to become a reliable source of knowledge,

---

[14] Indisputable: indubitable or beyond doubt; noninferential: something that is directly known and not inferred from other knowledge.

[15] Immanuel Kant, "What Is Enlightenment?," *Practical Philosophy*, trans. and ed. Mary J. Gregor (Cambridge, UK: Cambridge University Press, 1996), http://www.marxists.org/reference/subject /ethics/kant/enlightenment.htm (emphasis original). Note that the term *minority* means in this context the human being's immaturity or apprenticeship.

the right method was crucial. The Scientific Revolution became the prototype of what it meant to gather data in objective and uncorrupted form. Scientific knowledge of the physical universe through physics became the model of the proper pursuit of *all* knowledge. Scientific methods, it was presumed, were timeless and eternal, unencumbered by historical particularities, and the result of their application would be universally true knowledge.

Two additional developments had particular relevance to modern psychology. The first was the concept of the mechanical universe. Ironically, in its original form, the concept of a mechanical universe was proposed in the physical sciences in support and defense of traditional Christianity, specifically as an antidote to the magical universe of the Renaissance. Its most persuasive defender was the devoutly Christian chemist Robert Boyle, who believed the universe "behaved according to rules that God had freely chosen."[16] The laws of nature themselves were seen by Boyle as God-designed and an expression of divine sovereignty, activity, and wisdom. Later, though, the mechanical universe proved compatible with the absentee god of the deists and the nonexistent God of the atheists. It is "a great irony [that the] philosophy of nature that, during the seventeenth century, was upheld as the most protective of a sense of the sacred in nature was that very one that, in later social contexts, was most easily reinterpreted to support a subversive and secular creed."[17]

The second key mid-nineteenth-century development was Darwin's theory of evolution. In terms of the development of psychology, the most crucial implication of Darwin's theory of evolution was the blurring of the bright line between human and nonhuman life. Under the influence of Christian understandings, human uniqueness in distinction from the animals had been emphasized (and, as we shall see, perhaps in some ways overemphasized).

---

[16] Brooke, *Science and Religion*, 132; this is the contingency discussed earlier.
[17] Ibid., 118.

Darwin's theory broke down the bifurcation between human and nonhuman, opening up the possibility of the application to humans of principles derived from the study of animals (both physiologically and behaviorally).

In summary, we have emphasized five key elements of the Enlightenment:

1) The search through human reason alone for foundational truths that are indisputable and noninferential (thus creating a gulf between fact and opinion).

2) The rejection of religious tradition and authority as sources of sure knowledge, with reason becoming the locus and arbiter of knowledge (thus creating a vast gulf between reason and faith, fact and value).

3) Confidence in scientific methods to produce certain knowledge and the presumption that true knowledge will be ahistorical and universal (thus creating a vast gulf between knowledge by revelation and that coming by reason).

4) The triumph of a mechanistic conception of the cosmos (thus making God an extraneous variable unnecessary to the life of the mind).

5) The breakdown of any hard distinctions between human and nonhuman life (thus moving the human being from looking through the microscope to being the object of observation under the microscope).

PSYCHOLOGY: CHILD OF THE ENLIGHTENMENT

It is no coincidence that psychology as a science emerged at what could be regarded as the pinnacle of the Scientific Revolution and after the intellectual triumph of the Enlightenment; this is the intellectual context that has given us the field of psychology as we have it today. Psychology is commonly defined as the scientific study of mind, brain, and behavior, with "scientific study" presumed to exclude any appropriation of religious ideas as useful for understanding persons.

Introductory psychology textbooks commonly emphasize the empirical methods of study used in the field, the importance of accumulated evidence in making judgments, the applicability of findings in the animal kingdom for understanding human psychological characteristics, and the importance of neurological and genetic influences on human behavior. One subtle but important perspective offered throughout the field is the importance of analyzing all mental and behavioral phenomena in terms of their *function*; it is vital, it is argued, to analyze human phenomena in terms of their contribution to adaptation to the environment (survival) and to genetic propagation. Such a strategy is directly related to a Darwinian understanding of life, as Darwin emphasized natural selection of characteristics that served functional purposes.

In contrast to the cluster of presuppositions fostered by the Enlightenment, I suggest re-centering our thinking on Christian understandings of the human person and of the cosmos. Under such Christian understandings, a robust science is still possible, and so is productive conversation and engagement with secular scientific findings. Further, Christian perspectives open up new questions and new possibilities that are compelling. For instance, there is nothing intrinsically wrong and much to commend about analyzing human behavior in terms of its function. To quote C. S. Lewis, "The first qualification for judging any piece of workmanship from a corkscrew to a cathedral is to know *what* it is—what it was intended to do and how it is meant to be used."[18] But should we assume that survival and propagation are the key functions for understanding the purposes for which any human thought or behavior exists? To anticipate later arguments, I suggest that there is no need for Christians to deny the importance of survival and

---

[18] C. S. Lewis, *A Preface to Paradise Lost* (London: Oxford University Press, 1942), 1, emphasis original.

genetic propagation, but we will be led astray by the assumption that these are our *primary or only* purposes in existence.

AFTER THE ENLIGHTENMENT

Before moving forward, it is important to acknowledge that the Enlightenment (also called "Modernism") has lost some of its dominance in secular intellectual circles. The seeds for its decline were embedded there from the start. The core problem goes back to Descartes's pursuit of indisputable and noninferential knowledge. Simply put, there is no such knowledge. "The first step back from a commitment to [Enlightenment] rationalism is to acknowledge that we can never fully *decontextualize* philosophy or science. When we deal with intellectual or practical problems, we can never totally clean the slate, and start from scratch, as Descartes demands."[19]

It is commonly acknowledged among philosophers today that there is no such thing as pure, objective perception; rather, "all seeing is *seeing as . . .*" Everything we see is linked to other assumptions and perceptions that we have as human beings. Everything we know is part of a web of belief. As a result, any human assertion can be disputed; there is no such thing as indisputable human knowledge.

Some would take this to the extreme of relativism, but this is not a necessary step. Many are "critical realists" who recognize that humans can still know truly even if we have to take into account certain aspects of subjectivity and perspective in our human knowing.[20] Indeed, these weaknesses in the Enlightenment project have opened possibilities for thinking Christianly about psychology. There is broad recognition that instead of indisputable facts, the results of psychological study are instead facts as understood from a particular perspective. One clear and concise expression of

---

[19] Toulmin, *Cosmopolis*, 82.
[20] See Stanton L. Jones, "A Constructive Relationship for Religion with the Science and Profession of Psychology: Perhaps the Boldest Model Yet," *American Psychologist* 49 (1994).

this comes from respected psychologist of religion Ralph Hood, who has stated that any scientific "method is at least an implicit epistemology [a way of knowing], and any epistemology assumes at least an implicit ontology [an understanding of what is]. Simply put, how we seek to know assumes what we believe to be real."[21]

Thus, when presented with findings in the field of psychology, as in all areas of human inquiry, we owe appropriate deference to the findings as presented, but we also have room to ask whether the scientist has grounded her research in the best understanding of reality as it is and used the best way of knowing that reality in her research. This is particularly true given the complexity of what we study in the field of psychology. Human behavior and thought are unbelievably complex. When we gather data in this field, we focus in on a very limited part of our experience and exclude untold realms of other potential data. Thus, "psychologists may be likened to fishermen throwing their lines into an unexplored lake. What fish they catch depends upon the nature of the hook and of the bait used. It seems clear that a wise psychologist would bring with him a variety of hooks and bait, and try to be aware of his own limitations as a fisherman."[22]

It is this kind of wisdom that we seek as Christian thinkers in psychology: the wisdom to start with the right understandings—biblical understandings—as we approach the phenomena of human existence, the wisdom to seek the right methods for acquiring more detailed knowledge about the human condition, and the wisdom to engage respectfully and thoughtfully but assertively as we attempt to learn from the field of psychology.

In taking this approach, we are challenging and revising each of the five key elements of the Enlightenment presented earlier:

---

[21] Ralph Hood Jr., "Methodological Diversity in the Psychology of Religion and Spirituality," in *APA Handbook of Psychology, Religion, and Spirituality*, 2 vols., ed. Kenneth Pargament (Washington, DC: American Psychological Association, 2013), 1:79.
[22] Peter A. Bertocci, cited in Kenneth Pargament et al., "Envisioning an Integrative Paradigm for the Psychology of Religion and Spirituality, *APA Handbook*, 1:7.

1) We see the religious search for truth and the rational/scientific search for truth as complementary and intertwined and acknowledge that all knowing is grounded in some sort of faith.

2) We accept religious tradition and authority as a source of sure knowledge of certain kinds.

3) We evidence confidence tempered by humility in our celebration of religious truth and in truth discovered by scientific methods.

4) We celebrate the rationality of an ordered universe that can be studied even as God sustains it, guides it, and intervenes in it.

5) We acknowledge the creatureliness and physicality of human life, with many characteristics shared with subhuman creatures, even as humans are more than their physical bodies.

2

THE WORK OF INTEGRATION AND A CHRISTIAN VIEW OF PERSONS

Christianity is not first or primarily an intellectual system. Christianity is fundamentally a personal response to Jesus Christ, who invites each of us, "Follow me." Before the first followers were called "Christians" by others (Acts 11:26), they described themselves as followers of "the Way" (Acts 9:2). But the reason we can follow a crucified and risen Lord is that we *believe* Jesus Christ is Lord and Savior, the one true Son of God, and *believe* that this God—Father, Son, and Holy Spirit—has revealed himself and his will for our lives across the millennia through the prophets, preeminently through the teaching and life of Jesus Christ, and subsequently in the teachings of the apostles.

Thus, to follow Christ involves, in part, receiving and embracing a set of beliefs. These beliefs are about God, but they are also about us and our world. Because God is all-wise and all-knowing, Christians have historically believed that what God has revealed in the Bible about himself, us, and our world—called by theologians God's "special revelation"—forms a cohesive whole that *gives broad order and meaning to everything around us.* On the basis of God's truth, Christian truth, we begin to see reality as a cohesive whole. This is why many speak of a "Christian worldview."[1]

Christians throughout the ages have understood that receiving God's truth in faith provides a basis for seeing the totality of our lives differently and truthfully. Anselm of Canterbury, a millennium ago, wrote: "I do not attempt, O Lord, to penetrate Thy profundity, for I desire to understand in some degree Thy Truth, which my heart believes and loves. For I do not seek to understand, in order that I may believe; but *I believe that I may understand*. For I believe this too, that unless I believed, I should not understand."[2] More recently, C. S. Lewis reflected the same basic sentiment: "I believe in Christianity as I believe that the Sun has risen, not only because I see it but because by it I see everything else."[3]

It is only through the lens of Christian faith that we can see truly. But seeing truly is not a claim to human perfection or omniscience. We do not see everything perfectly, but by God's grace and through his revelation of truth, we have a chance to see rightly enough. It is important to emphasize the balance between Christian confidence in our grounding in God's revelation and a certain modesty and humility in asserting what we know.

On the one hand, it is not an act of arrogance to believe that God's Holy Word, the Bible, is completely true and can guide us to truth. It is another matter (and an error), however, to believe that our interpretations of God's Holy Word are certain or perfectly true. We err when we arrogantly believe that our interpretations of biblical truth are always right, whether those interpretations are applied to theological topics or to our understandings of the broader world.

It is equally problematic to believe that because God's Holy

[1] Philip G. Ryken, *Christian Worldview: A Student's Guide*, Recovering the Christian Intellectual Tradition (Wheaton, IL: Crossway, 2013).

[2] Mark A. Noll, *Jesus Christ and the Life of the Mind* (Grand Rapids, MI: Eerdmans, 2011), 47, emphasis added.

[3] C. S. Lewis, "Is Theology Poetry?," in *Essay Collection and Other Short Pieces*, ed. Lesley Walmsley (London: HarperCollins, 2000), 21.

Word is *completely true* that it is also *truly complete*. We err when we push the revelations of truth God has given us in the Bible to a level of precision or comprehensiveness that God did not intend. To use an analogy, God's Word is a map that can guide us truly, but a map is different from actually traversing the territory it describes.[4] A map is always a summary, an approximation, even when it is trustworthy. A map that summarizes national and state highway systems will not contain detailed summaries of footpaths or bicycle paths. As we trace out the Christian foundations for an understanding of human beings, we will find much that we do not know (and wish we did). There are many questions that Scripture leaves unanswered or that only hint at an answer.

THE NATURE OF INTEGRATION

So what do we do with the guidance provided by God's Word as we approach an academic discipline such as psychology? We seek, I would argue, to integrate Christianity or Christian faith with psychology, which I have defined as follows:

> Integration of Christianity and psychology (or any area of "secular thought") is our living out—in this particular area—of the Lordship of Christ over all of existence by our giving his special revelation—God's true Word—its appropriate place of authority in determining our fundamental beliefs about and practices toward all of reality and toward our academic subject matter in particular.[5]

There are many Christian intellectuals pursuing this same task. Christian philosophers J. P. Moreland and Francis Beckwith offer a longer, complementary definition, which makes a distinc-

---

[4] There are limitations to any analogy applied to Scripture or other divine mysteries. Any map, for instance, converts a multidimensional reality into a static, two-dimensional representation and thus is necessarily distorted. An alternative analogy might be that the statement "π = 3.14" is a truthful approximation but one that is not completely true because it does not convey the infinite extension of this number; so also the Bible is true but does not exhaust all knowledge.

[5] Stanton Jones, "An Integration View," in *Psychology and Christianity: Five Views*, 2nd ed., ed. Eric L. Johnson (Downers Grove, IL: InterVarsity, 2010), 102.

tion between conceptual and personal integration implicit in my definition:

> There are two kinds of integration: conceptual and personal. In *conceptual integration*, one's theological beliefs, especially those arrived at from careful study of the Bible, are blended and unified with important reasonable ideas from one's profession or college major into a coherent, intellectually satisfying Christian worldview. As Augustine wisely advised, "we must show our Scriptures not to be in conflict with whatever [our critics] can demonstrate about the nature of things from reliable sources." In *personal integration*, one seeks to live a unified life; a life in which he or she is the same in public as in private; a life in which the various aspects of his or her personality are consistent with each other and conducive to a life of human flourishing as a disciple of Jesus.[6]

If conceptual or academic integration is giving God's special revelation its appropriate place of authority in determining our fundamental beliefs about and practices toward our academic subject matter, what are our practical steps forward? We start by examining what God's Word says that is of relevance to psychology, namely, Christianity's crucial truths about human beings and the context in which we live.

A CHRISTIAN VIEW OF EVERYTHING

We begin at the broadest possible level because it is important to get our bearings as we embark on a complex journey. To understand anything, we must understand Christ. In the words of one of the most distinguished Christian intellectuals today, Mark Noll:

> The Trinity—Father, Son, and Spirit in the Unity of the Godhead—provides the essential, if also deeply mysterious, starting

[6] J. P. Moreland and Francis J. Beckwith, "Series Preface: A Call to Integration and the Christian Worldview Integration Series," in John H. Coe and Todd W. Hall, *Psychology in the Spirit: Contours of a Transformational Psychology* (Downers Grove, IL: InterVarsity, 2010), 11–12, emphasis original.

point [for pursuing human learning]. Other aspects of Christian faith also play a part in human learning: for example, the divine creation of the world, the fact of human sinfulness, God's merciful resolve to rescue sinners, the convicting work of the Holy Spirit, and the providential oversight of everything that ever takes place. Yet intrinsic to all such Christian realities are the person of Christ and the meaning of his work for all humanity in all human history. To understand that person and to fathom that work is to approach the center of Christianity itself.[7]

The very nature of God, the Trinitarian Father, Son, and Holy Spirit, provides the broadest context for our Christian understanding of humanity. The person of Christ is equally central in understanding what it means to be human, because he was and is the one perfect and enduring representation of what humanity truly is and was meant to be.

In addition to invoking the nature of God, Noll also speaks about understanding "the meaning of his work for all humanity." To understand humanity, we must understand the *narrative of redemption*. Scripture gives us an extraordinarily broad lens through which to see all of existence. Many Christian traditions summarize this broad narrative of redemption as the essential structure of a Christian worldview. In this understanding, there are four great "acts" in the "play" of cosmic history as we know it: creation, fall, redemption, and consummation.[8] This narrative is not simply *a* story; it is *the* story. As theologian Robert Jensen has stated it: "Scripture's story is not part of some larger narrative; it is itself the larger narrative of which all of the true narratives are parts."[9]

Everything—humanity, the animal kingdom, material reality, the world of the supernatural—is part of a divine drama that began with creation as described in Genesis 1 and 2. Returning to

---

[7] Noll, *Jesus Christ and the Life of the Mind*, ix.
[8] Summarized by Ryken in *Christian Worldview*.
[9] Robert Jensen, in David Dockery and Timothy George, *The Great Tradition of Christian Thinking: A Student's Guide*, Reclaiming the Christian Intellectual Tradition (Wheaton, IL: Crossway, 2012), 62.

Mark Noll's urging that we consider the centrality of Christ, it is important to note that the New Testament teaches that Christ himself, as a full member of the Trinity, was the creator and continues to be the sustainer and providential guide of all of creation (John 1; Colossians 1). After the creation, everything fell apart as a result of the fall—the rebellion of Satan and his minions and then our human rebellion in the garden of Eden (Genesis 3)—with the result that the entire cosmos has been corrupted and tainted by evil and rebellion against the Most High God.

But God in Christ was not content to allow us to plunge into corruption without hope; even at the end of Genesis 3 we are given a glimmer of hope for redemption in a promised Messiah, the coming Savior. We have a disease, but there is a cure. The groundwork is laid for that redemption through God's faithful, covenantal engagement with the people of Israel (and through them, the world), which began to take its final form in the birth of the promised Messiah, Jesus. Redemption reached its culmination in the crucifixion of Christ and his triumph over death and the grave. We live now, after the offering of this final redemption, and are beginning the work of the accomplishment of the consummation as we seek to spread Christ's kingdom throughout all the earth. The final consummation, however, awaits the second return of the risen Lord Christ.

This way of looking at the universe shifts us from seeing reality as a chaotic sequence of meaningless events to understanding that there is a dramatic trajectory to all of existence. Everything matters, because everything is part of God's work in redeeming a broken cosmos. Dockery and George discuss an important implication of this conviction, that "no object in nature, and no event in history, is an isolated, opaque fact closed in on itself. Each is, rather, a translucent window into a whole pattern of human experience."[10] And further, this dramatic character of existence entails an understanding that the universe is intrinsically moral,

---

[10] Dockery and George, *Great Tradition of Christian Thinking*, 62.

laden with value. Values are not something that human subjectivity projects on the universe (reality is neutral; only humans impute value), but rather value infuses the universe because everything is part of God's redemptive work.

One more caution: we need to realize the complexity and mystery of the nature of God and the nature of the human beings who are made in his image. Noll emphasizes that the Christian truth is often immensely complex and puzzling. He emphasizes the strong elements of paradox, duality, complexity, and multiplicity in understanding God and humanity. Noll quotes from John R. W. Stott on Christ's sacrifice on the cross, that "the cross was an act simultaneously of punishment and amnesty, severity and grace, justice and mercy." Regarding our human condition, Stott ponders similar complexities: "Who am I? . . . I am both noble and ignoble, beautiful and ugly, good and bad, upright and twisted, image and child of God, and yet sometimes yielding obsequious homage to the devil from whose clutches Christ has rescued me. My true self is what I am by creation, which Christ came to redeem, and by calling. My false self is what I am by the Fall, which Christ came to destroy."[11] We strike out into matters far beyond our mastery in reflecting on where we come from, who we are, what we are, and where we are going.

A CHRISTIAN VIEW OF PERSONS

The Bible is filled from cover to cover with direct instruction and teaching about how to live our lives. Scattered liberally throughout the Scriptures is much that is relevant to the applied aspects of the field of psychology: moral instruction, proverbial wisdom, prophetic exhortation, instructions for how to order our inner and communal lives, and on and on. But when it comes to the great truths that would provide guidance to us as we think about the questions that intrigue psychologists, we need to step back and

---

[11] John Stott, quoted in Noll, *Jesus Christ and the Life of the Mind*, 70.

distill some of the wisdom offered by a particular subfield of Christian theology, theological anthropology (the teachings/doctrines of what it means to be human).

MADE IN THE IMAGE OF GOD

Genesis 1:26 contains the very first biblical truth that we learn about human existence: "Then God said, 'Let us make man in our image, after our likeness.'" The first, deepest, most fundamental truth that we can affirm about humanity is that all of us—not just males, not just one race, not just royalty, not just those who are born or have matured to a certain age, not just those who meet up to certain standards of performance or autonomy—*all* of humanity is made in the image of God (in the Latin, *imago Dei*).

What does this mean? In the ancient Near East at the time of the writing of Genesis, images were used to represent the authority of and mark out the territory of a deity or of a king (and in many cultures, the king was presumed to be a deity). When kings conquered territories, they ordered images of themselves or of their god(s) set up to mark their territory and establish their authority. In most of the creation narratives told by the pagan people surrounding the Israelites, only one person or one family—the king and/or the royal family—was created in the image of a god. Commoners had been created for labor to serve the king. In these cultures, the idea of women being made in the divine image was inconceivable; many of these creation stories describe women as a result of a cataclysm, a joke, a mistake, or a war.

The teaching of Genesis is utterly different. *All of humanity is of divine descent.* In this context, the first two of the Ten Commandments begin to make sense. The first commandment is to have no other gods besides the one true God. The very next commandment is to refrain from making graven images of the divine. How are these two commandments connected? There is only one true God, and there is no need to make images of him because he has already made images of himself in the person of every human being. We see the image of the divine as we look at each other.

Among many other critical truths, we must understand that to be made in the image of God means that every human being is a person of infinite value. In our society that so often values persons by what they can do, by what they can earn, or by their appearance, we learn from the doctrine of the image of God that every person is of infinite value.

But what concretely *is* the image of God? What is it about me and you that reflects God? Unfortunately, the Scriptures offer no tight description or definition, and this matter has been debated for millennia. The main views can be summarized as follows.[12]

- *The Image as Substance.* Some have argued that being made in the image of God means being made of certain kinds of constituent elements. The classic arguments have said that we are made in the image of God because, like him, we are made of soul or spirit.

- *The Image as Capacity.* Some have argued that the image is a capacity or set of capacities essential to what it means to be human. The classic arguments have included that what sets us apart is our capacities for rationality, self-reflection, language, volition, and/or the capacity to worship.

- *The Image as Function.* Some have argued that it is what we do or are called to do that makes us in the image of God. Images in the ancient world serve particular functions; thus, our being in the image of God must be found in our responsibility to represent God to the world, or exercising dominion on his behalf over creation, or worshiping the one true God, or some such purpose.

- *The Image as Relationality.* Due to difficulties with the other arguments and the fact that all of them seem to contain certain essential

---

[12] Combining the views of James Beck and Bruce Demarest, *The Human Person in Theology and Psychology: A Biblical Anthropology for the 21st Century* (Grand Rapids, MI: Kregel, 2005) and Marc Cortez, *Theological Anthropology: A Guide for the Perplexed* (New York: T & T Clark International, 2010).

elements, a great deal of recent theological attention has focused on our capacity for relationship. Karl Barth articulated this view, saying: "Man is created by God in correspondence with this relationship and differentiation in God Himself: created as a Thou that can be addressed by God but also an I responsible to God; in the relationship of man and woman in which man is a Thou to his fellow and therefore himself and I in responsibilities to this claim."[13] Barth argues that the one true God is a relational God by his very essence because he is Trinitarian, and that he intentionally made human beings relational in his image both in a vertical direction (responsiveness to God) and in a horizontal direction (as male and female).

Pondering and wrestling with understanding the meaning of humanity being made in the image of God is foundational to understanding humanity, including human psychology. But there are other emphases of Scripture that bear separate elaboration.

EMBODIED, GENDERED, AND SEXUAL SOULS

One of the deficiencies of the idea of the image of God as our being composed of soul or spirit is its failure to acknowledge God's intentional creation of humanity as physical, embodied beings. We are made out of the dust of the earth. We are part of physical creation, not an alien intrusion into creation.

Two common problems get in the way of the proper embrace and celebration of humanity as embodied. First, some Christians underemphasize our embodiment because they misunderstand New Testament instructions to deny or crucify the flesh. This instruction is not directed toward our physical bodies. Instead, in this context the term "the flesh" refers not to our physical bodies but to our sinful, rebellious nature, a nature that penetrates and contaminates all aspects of our personhood—body, mind, soul, emotions, and will. Second, some Christians fail to realize the significance of physical existence for both the person of Jesus

---

[13] Karl Barth, quoted in Cortez, *Theological Anthropology*, 24.

Christ and the afterlife. The Bible teaches that Jesus really was an embodied human whose embodiment continues permanently; even at God's right hand he is a glorified and embodied Christ. So it is that we also will have an embodied, resurrected, everlasting existence.

Our embodiment includes our gendered natures and our sexuality. God did not create generic, androgynous, sexually undifferentiated humanity, but rather male and female. God blessed the union of Adam and Eve, celebrating the fact that they would "be fruitful and multiply and fill the earth" (Gen. 1:28).

In contrast to some other religious worldviews, particularly a Buddhist worldview that views embodiment as intrinsically evil and/or deficient, the Christian understanding celebrates embodiment. In fact, it is not too strong to say that we *are* bodies; we are more than bodies, but we *are* bodies. Just as you, the reader, are either male or female and yet more than male or female, so also you are your body but are more than your body. That *more* is what Christians call the "soul" or the "spirit." The Bible appears to use the terms *soul* and *spirit* to refer to an immaterial part or dimension of our existence that sets us apart, in certain ways, from the physical world. I summarize this by describing us as "embodied souls."

Even so, human beings were created as part of the broader work of creation of the cosmos. Because we are embodied, we participate materially and necessarily in the stuff of the physical world. The Scriptures do not deny that we share many qualities with other animals. In fact, the Bible does not deny that we *are* animals; we are animals even as simultaneously we are more than animals.

In chapter 1 I spoke critically of the dominance of Darwinian naturalism and its erosion of any bright line between humanity and the animal kingdom. If human beings are made uniquely in the image of God, then there is indeed a bright line between human and animal. But this bright line is also a porous line, one that allows us also to acknowledge a great deal of shared physical and even mental characteristics with other animals. We are unique but not in every way.

RELATIONAL BEINGS

In the second telling of the creation story in Genesis 2, we learn that the first man, Adam, was created perfect, resided in the perfect world not yet sullied and poisoned by sin, was given the perfect job of tending the garden, and rested in perfect relationship with the perfect Lord of this creation. And in all of this perfection, there was one thing that was "not good," namely, "that the man should be alone" (v. 18). Humanity was made for horizontal relationship to others, and to one special other, as well as for vertical relationship to God.

Our sexuality is not just a manifestation of our embodiment, and it is certainly more than a mere mechanism by which human beings can procreate. Ephesians 5 teaches that to think about marriage is to think about Christ's love for his church. Our sexuality is a finite reflection of God's infinite, perfect love and relatedness. Because of that, marriage on this earth is a heavenly symbol or image of the loving God's relationship to his people. Marriages were meant to be signposts to a watching world, as another manifestation of the image of God symbolizing the faithfulness and passion of God's love for his people.

But relationality is not just manifest in marriages; single persons as well—single persons like the Lord Jesus Christ himself—can manifest richly our relationality as intended by God. The gendered and sexual nature of every person, whether married or not, teaches us that we are made for relationships, for love and for giving. Single persons show their love for God in their obedience to God's moral guidance for manifestation of their sexuality and in their deep connections with and service to others.

RESPONSIBLE BEINGS

Responsibility has two dimensions. First, it is notable that human beings were created to work. In Genesis 1 they are charged to exercise dominion over the earth in God's stead, to rule like a steward on behalf of the true king. In Genesis 2 we are told specifically Adam is given the creative charge to name and thus classify the entire animal kingdom, a great intellectual challenge, and that Adam and Eve were to tend the garden of Eden. Human beings, thus, are purposeful beings, designed to fulfill God's purposes here on earth through meaningful work.

Combined with relationality, this facet of responsibility gives us clues to fundamental human motivations. I have speculated elsewhere that the twin blessings and exhortations of Genesis 2 to cultivate and keep the garden of Eden (v. 15) and to become one flesh (v. 24) suggest that human beings are made with two fundamental motivations in life:

1) Significance: "A human need for purposeful activity in life, and need for meaningful work in the realization of purpose outside of ourselves"; and

2) Relatedness: a human need for "meaningful relationships characterized by intimacy and unity even while we celebrate our uniqueness."[14]

But there is a second dimension of responsibility: we are morally responsible for our actions. God throughout Scripture treats human beings in such a way that shows they have real choice. Adam and Eve were given a choice of eternal moral significance: they were commanded not to eat of the fruit of the tree of the knowledge of good and evil. The resulting punishment for their disobedience inflicted by God indicates that they were held morally culpable for

---

[14] Stanton L. Jones and Richard E. Butman, *Modern Psychotherapies: A Comprehensive Christian Appraisal*, 2nd ed. (Downers Grove, IL: InterVarsity, 2011), 75, 77.

making the wrong choice, the choice of disobedience and rebellion. To be a human is to share in their moral culpability.

We, like they, have responsibility or agency. In the words of philosopher C. Stephen Evans, "Human beings are first and foremost agents. Their lives do not merely consist of a string of happenings or events, but constitute a series of choices and decisions about what they will do." Or, in the words of C. S. Lewis, "for us as rational creatures, to be created also means 'to be made agents.' We have nothing that we have not received; but part of what we have received is the power of being something more than receptacles."[15] Human beings have freedom. There may be limits on this freedom, as we will discuss in the next two chapters, but we have freedom of a meaningful sort. One implication of this is, in the thought of Pope John Paul II, "to be a human is to be a moral agent [which means, in turn,] that we live in a human universe the very structure of which is dramatic. In the great drama of any life is the struggle to surrender the person-I-am to the person-I-ought-to-be."[16]

BROKEN BEINGS

The consensual teaching of the Christian church has been that humans are necessarily sinful; this is the doctrine of original sin, the teaching that we are born into sin. The related doctrine of total depravity is the teaching that sin contaminates every part of human existence. This latter doctrine is often misunderstood as teaching that human beings are entirely evil, that we are always as bad as we could possibly be. This is an obvious misunderstanding, because anyone with any imagination can imagine themselves being more wicked than they are currently. Total depravity does not mean that we are fundamentally evil, because as beings made in the image of God, we see sin as something layered on top of our basic good

---

[15] C. Stephen Evans and C. S. Lewis, quoted in ibid., 71.
[16] From George Weigel, *Witness to Hope: The Biography of Pope John Paul II* (New York: Harper Perennial, 2001), 8.

nature. Because sin has contaminated our entire being (like a drop of ink disperses throughout a glass of pure water), it touches everything. Total depravity means our motivations are intermingled with that which is twisted and evil to varying degrees; good intentions go awry.

The witness of Scripture about the nature of sin is very complex. Sometimes the word *sin* refers to specific acts: "that action of theft was a sin." Sometimes the word *sin* refers to a disposition, as when Scripture describes the "sin nature." The sinful disposition is toward specific acts, but it is also tinged with a spirit of rebellion and enmity against God. Yet again, Scripture sometimes describes sin as something beyond ourselves, a power or force that keeps us enslaved and pushes us in the direction of rebellion against God (e.g., Romans 6–7). Understanding the complex reality of sin is necessary if we are to understand human nature.

And thanks to the work of Christ on the cross, we can be redeemed and justified and make significant movement toward freedom from sin.

CONCLUSION

I have just begun to sketch the richness of the field of theological anthropology. The Christian view of persons is complex and, to a certain extent, incomplete and mysterious, leaving many questions unanswered. We can be hopeful about further enlightenment as we approach the discipline of psychology for a fruitful conversation about what it means to be human. But unbelieving thinkers in the discipline approach their subject matter making certain assumptions about the basic character of human existence, views that structure and shape all the scientific data that result from their subsequent careful examinations. We will be seeking to understand those assumptions and how they are different from and similar to Christian assumptions in what follows.

Christians believe that we are all part of the same family and that we share certain basic characteristics common to all. As individuals, we can be wildly and profoundly different from each other, but underneath those differences lie the commonalities that tie us together as family. It is essential that we reflect on these common characteristics as we move into the study of psychology.

+ 3

NEUROSCIENCE, EMBODIMENT, AND MIND

September 13, 1848, was a bad day for Phineas Gage.[1] A dependable railroad foreman, he was leading a crew cutting through the rocky hills of Vermont to make way for the railroad line. Their routine was for a member of the team to drill a hole in the rock, put explosive powder with a fuse in the hole, and add sand as a buffer. Then Gage's job was to tamp the mixture down with a rod, retreat to a safe distance, and ignite the explosion. His tamping rod was 3 feet 7 inches long, weighed 13.5 pounds, had a blunt tamping end more than 1 inch in diameter, and tapered to a point at the other end.

Apparently distracted momentarily, Gage slammed the rod into the hole before the sand had been added, igniting the explosion instantly. The hole in the rock functioned like a rifle barrel and the tamping rod became a gigantic bullet, slamming pointed end first into the underside of his left cheekbone, then passing through his left eye socket, and exiting through the top of his head, leaving a crater of broken skull several inches wide. It landed about 30 yards behind him.

Gage was stunned but never lost consciousness. Minutes after, he was able to speak lucidly and rationally and could walk under his own power. The doctor who examined him hours after the accident apparently found him drinking lemonade and capable of

---

[1] Drawing here from the best source on Gage: Malcolm Macmillan, *The Phineas Gage Information Page* (1999–2012), http://www.uakron.edu/gage (accessed June 4, 2014).

answering questions even though much of the front part of the left side of his brain had been destroyed. The following describes his status after he returned to full strength:

> Some months after the accident, probably in about the middle of 1849, Phineas felt strong enough to resume work. But because his personality had changed so much, the contractors who had employed him would not give him his place again. Before the accident he had been their most capable and efficient foreman, one with a well-balanced mind, and who was looked on as a shrewd smart business man. He was now, [his doctor] Harlow said, fitful, irreverent, and grossly profane, showing little deference for his fellows. He was also impatient and obstinate, yet capricious and vacillating, unable to settle on any of the plans he devised for future action. His friends said he was "No longer Gage."[2]

The case of Phineas Gage is one of the first case studies in modern medicine to connect identifiable and serious brain injury with subsequent changes in personality. The case fueled interest in the relationship between the brain and personality. The best account of his later life is that after a period of instability, Gage slowly regained his hold on something of a normal existence. He earned a living first by exhibiting himself and lecturing as one of "The World's Greatest Wonders," a man who had "His Brains Blown Out" (as reads a flyer from 1852). As he exhausted this opportunity, he became a stagecoach driver. Toward the end of his life, he began to experience seizures and a deterioration of his adjustment. He suffered an unexplained premature death eleven years after his accident.

THE EMERGENCE OF CONTEMPORARY NEUROSCIENCE

A good bit of contemporary psychology is driven by neuroscience. As the wealth of information about the functioning of the brain

---

[2] Ibid.

and the broader nervous system grows, its applicability to our understanding of human behavior, emotion, personality, dysfunction, and other phenomena has exploded.

In antiquity, the functioning of the mind was extraordinarily mysterious and its relationship to the physical brain highly disputed. Ancient accounts of the "location" of the mental, emotional, and spiritual facets of the person vary. The brain itself is not referenced in the Bible, which varyingly seems to attribute psychological functions to the heart, the kidneys, and even the bowels. This does not mean that the Bible was or is in error, or that these organs actually perform cognitive functions, but rather is a manifestation of the Bible utilizing the thought forms and language of the people to communicate divine truth as God accommodated his revelation to what his people could and needed to hear. Just as we speak of the sun rising even though we know it is caused by the earth rotating, so also a biblical reference to feelings or motivations in "the heart" is a figure of speech, not a scientific formulation.

Science made only slow progress between antiquity and the modern period in understanding the relationship of mind and brain. In the early nineteenth century Franz Gall and Johann Spurzheim proposed the theory of phrenology, a speculative assignment of very specific personality traits to very specific locations in the brain, with the corollary assumption that aspects of personality could be detected by measuring bumps on the human skull caused by the relative size of each brain area related to those traits. Other scientists at the time were highly critical and proposed in contrast that the brain functions as a cohesive, diffuse, and completely integrated unit with almost no localized function. Neither approach was right.

In the late 1800s and early 1900s, experiments on animals in which specific brain regions were destroyed (ablated) began to suggest some localization of function. Destruction of one brain area might cause blindness, another paralysis in specific parts of the body, and yet others disruptions in learning, sensation, awareness, and so forth. It was at about this time that the accident of Phineas Gage suggested that despite the bankruptcy of phrenology as a theory, certain aspects of personality had connections to specific brain regions.

Recent scientific progress has been nothing short of staggering in advancing our understanding of the functioning of the brain in coordination with the central and peripheral nervous systems in connection to the entire body. The applications of this research in recent years are also astounding. Early applications included electroconvulsive therapy for depression and split-brain procedures to control the most devastating forms of epileptic seizures. More recent reports have included breakthroughs in inserting cochlear implants that allow the deaf to hear and retinal implants that allow limited sight to the blind and new capacities to implant chips in the brain of amputees, giving them the ability to manipulate robotic limbs in a way that promises to restore direct functionality. Similarly, advances in the understanding and synthesis of basic neurotransmitters are revolutionizing treatment of certain disorders.

I will make no attempt to summarize the functioning of individual neurons, specific areas of the brain, or their relationship to voluntary movement, learning, memory, consciousness or other functions; this information is available to the reader in any introduction to psychology textbook. But the recent discovery of "mirror neurons" can serve as a useful case study.

MIRROR NEURONS

Scientists have known for decades that specific neuron bundles are finely tuned to particular tasks. For instance, studies of the areas of the brain that process vision have discovered that neurons transmit signals from the three types of cone sensors in the retina responding to specific neurologically primary colors of light (blue, green, and red). These impulses are passed to the retinal ganglion cells, which begin to integrate and process this information, transmitting complex syntheses to yet more sophisticated processing centers in the occipital region of the brain at the back of the skull. Certain other neuron clusters process specialized information such as horizontal lines, vertical lines, and diagonal lines, and even the recognition of human faces.

The discovery of mirror neurons has further heightened interest in the specialization of aspects of the brain. It has long been known that animals can learn by observation. Dogs can learn a specific location for food by observing other dogs finding hidden treats. Is there a neurological explanation for such learning? Experimental studies with monkeys with sensory electrodes implanted in their brains revealed activation of specific neuronal pathways as the implanted observer monkey observed another (model) monkey engaging in certain types of behavior. Whereas in the last paragraph I was speaking about the specialization we see in the *visual* systems of the brain, these new pathways were detected in a different part of the brain, primarily among the neuronal tracts dedicated to muscular movement. Two things were especially intriguing about these findings.

First, the pathways that were activated overlapped with portions of the exact same neurological pathways that would have been activated had the observer monkey engaged in the same behavior (*mirrored* the behavior) himself! Second, this neurological response in the mirror neuron pathways was clearest and strongest when the behavior being observed was goal-directed behavior that was highly likely to be motivating to the observing monkey. For example, a hungry observer monkey watching a model monkey pick up a bowl and eat food from it demonstrated activation of largely the same neurological pathways that the observer monkey would have used had it engaged in the behavior itself.

Recent research has suggested the existence of similar mirror neuron systems in human beings. In these studies, humans are not subjected to electrode implantation but while watching video images are scanned by various types of functional imaging that allow revolutionary measurement of areas of brain activation from outside the skull.[3] The researchers set up complex experimental situations where, for instance, a thirsty human subject would see a meaningful action sequence such as a hand reaching into a complicated place setting on a table, picking up a glass of water, and setting the glass back down empty. Such a sequence would strongly activate the mirror neuron system, many of the same ones that would have been activated in the subject him- or herself had the subject been picking up, drinking from, and setting the glass back down. But when disjointed segments of the same actions were displayed, such as the hand simply moving empty tableware around, there was minimal activation of the mirror system. Similarly, experiments showed strong activation of mirror neuron systems when subjects were shown video clips of humans moving their jaws, in one case ingesting food and in the other case talking. They demonstrated much less activation when seeing similar videos of monkeys or dogs moving their jaws.

Researchers argue that in humans and monkeys, these mirror neurological systems are "linked to *understanding the meaning of the actions of others*."[4] Clearly, this research is a huge step forward. But do we completely understand observational learning in all its complexity now that we know some of the brain circuits that are involved in this important human capacity?

THE PROBLEM OF REDUCTIONISM

The progressive localization of more and more functions to specific brain regions has given new fuel to the classic problem in the field of psychology of *reductionism*: the claim that because a certain human experience involves certain simpler or more basic

[3] Positron Emission Tomography (PET) or functional Magnetic Resonance Imaging (fMRI).
[4] Giacomo Rizzolatti and Corrado Sinigaglia, *Mirrors in the Brain: How Our Minds Share Actions and Emotions* (New York: Oxford University Press, 2008), 124, emphasis original.

(often called more parsimonious) processes such as neurological pathways, then the more complex phenomenon can be reduced to or is "nothing but" the complex interaction of those more basic functions (e.g., nothing but the actions of those neurological pathways). With the incredible advances in neuroscience, it is increasingly assumed that all that we hold dear as uniquely human is "nothing but" the actions of the brain systems. As one example of neurological reductionism, the famous scientist who codiscovered the structure of DNA, Francis Crick, said "You're nothing but a pack of neurons."[5]

Of course, scientific reductionism does not stop at the level of the neuron. Some assume that every complex phenomenon can be completely reduced to the actions of lower-level systems. If mental functions can be explained completely in terms of neurological interactions, then in turn these too can be explained completely in terms of molecular interactions, which in turn can be explained completely in terms of atomic interactions, which in turn can finally be explained completely in terms of subatomic particle interactions via some yet to be determined elemental theory.

Increasingly our popular media contributes to this tendency toward reductionism in the form of what some have called "neuro-essentialism," the attribution of "subjectivity and personal identity to the brain. . . . Headline examples of this phenomenon are: 'Brain can banish unwanted memories,' 'how brain stores languages' and 'brain stores perceptions into small meaningful chunks.'"[6] Is it brains that do these things, or is it people? A neuro-essentialist view suggests that who we are as persons is ultimately reducible to our brains. When we engage in reductionism, the entity that is acting is no longer the human being but the human being's brain.

Neurological reductionism is not the only kind of reductionism. As the processes of animal learning were becoming more

---

[5] Francis Crick, *The Astonishing Hypothesis: The Scientific Search for the Soul* (New York: Scribner, 1984), 3.
[6] Eric Racine, et al., "fMRI in the Public Eye," Nature Reviews: *Neuroscience* 6 (2005): 160.

clearly understood, behaviorists argued strenuously that human behavior is nothing but the complex result of such basic learning processes. As Freud developed his theory of psychoanalysis, he argued that all forms of civilized human behavior could be reduced to the balancing of more primitive urges. These were bold claims.

MIND AND BRAIN

One of the great debates in human intellectual history is the relationship of mind and brain. The classical positions in the debate are that of the monists and the dualists.[7] Classical dualism suggests that there are two fundamental substances to human existence: our physical substance and some other nonphysical substance (whether we call it "mind," "soul," or "spirit"). Many Christians have been drawn to dualism. Augustine of Hippo, some sixteen hundred years ago, sought to defend the idea of an independent material soul by asking how the human mind, wherever it is housed in the body, could be understood as a mere physical entity to contain "abstract propositions, the principles of numbers and dimensions . . . false arguments, the . . . idea of God."[8] How could our minds have such capacities if they are not more than material?

The classic problem for dualism, however, is the challenge of explaining how these two different substances can interact and influence each other if they really are fundamentally different. Further, as evidence mounts that the physical processes of the brain fundamentally determine our mental experience (whether this be the experience of Phineas Gage or the evidence regarding the existence and functioning of mirror neurons), the more challenging it becomes to cling to dualism.

In contrast, monism suggests that there is just one substance. While there have been some nonphysical monists who have sug-

[7] See Marc Cortez, *Embodied Souls, Ensouled Bodies: An Exercise in Christological Anthropology and Its Significance for the Mind/Body Debate* (New York: T & T Clark, 2008).
[8] Stephen Rose, "Human Agency in the Neurocentric Age," *European Molecular Biology Organization Reports* 6 (2005): 1004.

gested that material reality is ultimately illusory and that there is only one "mental" substance that is ultimately real, these views have never really garnered much support in the West. On the other hand, physical monism—the belief that physical realities comprise all of the substance of our human existence—has been around since the ancient Greeks and has garnered tremendous support from contemporary neuroscience. But physical monism is not without its problems also. Most importantly, if our mental experiences are nothing but the firings of our neurons, then in what meaningful sense can we be said to actually apprehend what is true outside of ourselves? And in what sense can we be understood to be meaningfully free?

AN INTEGRATIVE INQUIRY

In chapter 2 I argued that in Christian perspective we are embodied beings, but we are more than bodies. We need to clear away a prejudice sometimes manifested by some Christians: based on the correct presumptions that humans have or are spirits and souls and that we have some sort of freedom, some Christians go further with a seeming prejudice against the importance of our bodies. This prejudice generates incredulity toward the kind of findings coming from the field of neuroscience. We need to get over our prejudice against the importance of our bodies. As discussed in chapter 2, we are, at a profound level, *embodied beings* with all that entails. We may be more than our bodies, but we are, in part, our bodies. We have limitations, including the limitations imposed by our embodied nature.

But if we are more than our bodies, then by extension it would seem that our brains may be fundamental to what it means to be persons but that we are more than the firings of our neurons. There are allies in the secular neuroscience community arguing similarly, that we are more than just our bodies, more than just our neurons. Neuroscientist William Hurlbut notes that naturalistic and reductionistic views fail to satisfy us; "there is a sense that what is most important and distinctly human has slipped through the fingers of the grasp of science. Somehow the new conceptions of human nature fall short of coherent with the fullness of life as actually lived and experienced. They fail to sustain our sense of irreducible personal identity, our capacity for free choice, and our commitment to ideals and transcendent truths."[9]

Is there room for mind, soul, and/or spirit, and for limited freedom? The idea of *emergentism*—an idea advocated by a number of philosophers and scientists[10]—is that as more, complex fundamental entities combine, in the words of neuroscientist Roger Sperry, they may produce "new, previously nonexistent, emergent properties, including the mental, that interact causally at their own higher level and also exert causal control from above downward."[11] His fundamental claim, then, is that new properties emerge in more complex systems that are not predictable strictly from the lower-level components that make up the new system.

There is precedent in the natural world to think that this may be possible. Water, for example, has properties that are not explicable from the characteristics of the oxygen and hydrogen atoms alone that make it up, such as the unique property of water expanding as it freezes (which is so unlike other molecular compounds). Combine rubber molecules with other substances to make an automobile tire, and the unique properties of the tire, such as rolling in a circular pattern, are not predictable from the properties of rubber molecules alone. Living cells are composed of a variety of complex molecules, but the properties unique to life are not fully explicable by the way nonliving molecules interact.

---

[9] William Hurlbut, "Science, Ethics, and the Human Spirit," in *The Oxford Handbook of Religion and Science* (New York: Oxford University Press, 2008), 872–73.

[10] I am using the term *emergentism* in this chapter not to advocate for the specific formulations of Roger Sperry for emergent "mind" but more generically for the idea that distinctly human capacities ("software") emerge from the biological "hardware" of our human condition.

[11] Roger Sperry, "Psychology's Mentalist Paradigm and the Religion/Science Tension," *American Psychologist* 43 (1988): 609.

Sperry does not deny that the cognitive functions of the human mind are completely dependent upon the basic brain processes that support it and that these in turn rely on the functions of molecules and atoms. When part of Phineas Gage's brain was destroyed, Gage irretrievably lost some of his mental functioning. But Sperry argues that mind is more than just these basic processes. He argues that "we and the universe are more than just swarms of 'hurrying' atoms, electrons, and protons, that the higher holistic properties and qualities of the world to which the brain responds, including all the macrosocial phenomena of modern civilization, are just as real and causal for science as are the atoms and molecules on which they depend."[12]

In other words, Sperry argues that humans manifest capacities as higher-level organisms that transcend and are not reducible to the more fundamental components that form a foundation for those capacities. These new capacities operate by rules that cannot be explained by the rules that govern the more foundational basis for the higher-order capacities. Thus, these capacities may constitute a reality—like "mind, spirit, or soul"—that transcends and yet is completely dependent, in the normal order of things, upon the biological systems that support it. I believe this begins to give us the framework for understanding how we can be fully embodied and yet more than our bodies.

Another preoccupation for those who have a Christian understanding of persons is the capacity we have for limited freedom. Sperry argues that some higher-order systems actually exert "causal control from above downward."[13] In the relationship of brain and mind, he argues that "mental states, as emergent properties of brain activity, thus exert downward control over their constituent neuronal events—at the same time that they are being determined by them."[14]

---

[12] Ibid.
[13] Ibid.
[14] Ibid.

If this is true, then far from being reducible to the constituent elements that form it, the human mind has powers of its own. Other neuroscientists agree that some move like this is essential; for instance, William Hurlbut has argued that "to account for all of human nature in terms of earlier evolutionary mechanisms ignores the evident freedom and emergence in nature. Human consciousness, symbolic language, and moral community are not fully described or understood by anything that has come before."[15] I will return to the issue of limited freedom again in the next chapter.

What does it mean for human uniqueness that we can learn so much from the study of animals? In chapter 2 I noted that human beings are animals, but we are more than animals. It is extraordinarily common today, however, for humans to be regarded as nothing but animals. We may be the most powerful or smartest animals and may excel on any number of other dimensions, but we are nevertheless *just* animals.

Christians of previous ages had often assumed that we were utterly different in our capacities from the animal kingdom. This categorical separation of humanity from the rest of living creation has been under assault from three directions. First, from a philosophical direction, the triumph of Enlightenment thinking and the wholesale embrace of Darwinian naturalism have undermined human uniqueness.

Second, scientific studies of an array of animal species with a variety of functional capacities have demonstrated that certain animal species (a) possess some capacities superior to those of human beings (as when some species can hear audio frequencies below or above our limited capacities, or can see parts of the visual spectrum beyond what we can) or (b) possess capacities previously thought to be completely unique to human beings (such as the rational and complex problem-solving capacities of higher primates or the complex social natures and capacities for self-awareness of dolphins).

---

[15] Hurlbut, "Human Agency," in *Oxford Handbook of Religion and Science*, 875.

Third, the knowledge we possess about fundamental capacities and characteristics of human beings has, without question, been vastly enriched by the comparative study across species of similar if more primitive capacities and characteristics of nonhuman species. One of the things that can be most troubling cumulatively to Christian studying at the university level—particularly in the field of psychology—is the avalanche of findings from the animal kingdom applicable to our understanding of humanity. Our encounter with such findings can contribute to the general sense that human beings are just animals after all.

I can here only begin to sketch a response to such a reaction, but I would urge the reader not to be discouraged or daunted by such findings. I reiterate, first, that though human beings are more than animals, we are animals and as such necessarily share in much that characterizes other living parts of God's created order.

Additionally, as many Christian leaders of the Scientific Revolution have reiterated, the entire created order, including human beings, bears the imprint of the creativity and intentions of the divine Creator. He is a creator who manifests remarkable diversity and creativity in what he made but who also manifests common elements of intentional design and function across the spectrum and diversity of his creation. One would expect clear elements of consistency in creation from a designer who is rational, intentional, logical, and consistent.

Christians beginning the study of psychology should embrace the rich array of findings that come from comparative study of animals for what they tell us about fundamental aspects of human neurological and other physical dimensions of our bodies as the "hardware" of what it means to be human. We can embrace such findings while being wary of reductionism that would conclude we are nothing but animals. The testimony of Scripture speaks to the contrary, but so also does a distinct voice inside of us, a voice that says there is something unique about every human being that transcends animal existence.

What are the implications of our profoundly biological nature for our capacity to know truly? Introductory psychology textbooks always have chapters on sensation and perception and on memory. These topics are among those in which the findings of neuroscience are invoked to expand our understanding of vital human capacities. These findings can challenge our presumption that human beings can know truly anything about their world and experience. In these areas and more, we confront the reality that human knowing is profoundly dependent upon our finite biology and also profoundly prone to limitations and tendencies toward errors. I will illustrate by focusing on the phenomenon of human memory.

External events impinge upon our nervous system, and some of the stimuli are encoded as sensory experiences. There is much that we do not encode; we are unaware of cosmic radiation because we have no sensory apparatus that can detect it, and we do not hear noises or see light above and below the frequencies that we can detect. From among the incredible array of external stimuli that impinge upon us, we detect certain ones and focus in to consciously experience an even smaller selection. A remarkable but finite amount of our experience is encoded as electrochemical signals by neurons connected to our sensory organs and passed on to other neurons as chemical signals across the tiny gaps between neurons called "synapses."

When these coded messages reach the parts of the brain involved in memory, a number of different processes occur. Some information is *automatically* processed without our conscious attention. We overlearn in certain areas, as when we are so accustomed to reading that we see certain complex visual patterns and just know, "Oh, there's the restroom!" Similarly, we automatically process elements of space and time such that when we realize that we do not have our cell phone, we effortlessly trace our steps back and realize, "Darn, I left it on the counter of the coffee shop ten minutes ago!" Some things automatically processed are almost immediately committed to long-term memory, such as events that are highly salient (think of that time that all of your friends screamed "Surprise!" as you came into the room) or of deep emotional significance (that time when the person you loved chose to crush your heart and walk away from the relationship).

Other types of information are processed and held in what psychologists call short-term memory and not retained in long-term memory. Almost all of us have had the experience of driving down a boring highway while listening to music, only to realize that we have no memory of the last forty-five minutes of the drive along the road. During that time, nevertheless, we saw cars, trucks, road signs, exits, and innumerable other things but are incapable of recalling them. They have not, in fact, been committed to memory and are gone forever.

Finally, certain kinds of information require what psychologists call "effortful processing." To remember the major points of this chapter, you may need to write out an outline or summary, rehearse the information, or engage in other deliberate strategies to master the material and move from passive reading to deliberate, long-term retention.

Memory is a profoundly biological phenomenon. And yet the exact nature of how memories are stored continues to elude us. What *is* a memory, biologically speaking? We know that memories are not converted to individual neurons and that memories are not converted into single complex molecules. We know which areas of the brain are most important to long- and short-term memory. But at the deepest level, we do not know what memories are.

The study of memory by neuroscientists and cognitive scientists also points out the limitations and peculiarities of memory. Memory processes are subject to patterns, even biases, that humble us. We know, for instance, that all events are not equal. Events that are highly evocative emotionally take priority and often become irreversibly and vividly lodged in human memory. Happy examples include the day our beloved proposed marriage or our wedding day; negative examples include the war veteran exposed to brutal conditions in combat or the victim of a fire or a rape. Such experiences can torment individuals, leading them to ask repeatedly, "Why can't I forget?"

I could just as easily have summarized the huge area of the study of sensation and perception, where again we encounter the profoundly biological and amazingly complex but limited and fallible capacities we have for awareness of the external world. I could have summarized the area of cognition, the study of how humans process information. As Christians contemplate such findings, we can become deeply troubled by the basic question of how, in the light of such findings, we can ever know anything truly. If what we know and how we think is subject to these biological limitations and the many demonstrated failings of our sensory, memory, and information-processing capacities, *isn't knowledge of truth a fundamental illusion*? Does the irrefutable demonstration of the finiteness and imperfection of our mental processes reinforce the postmodern idea of human knowledge as a subjective construction (chapter 1)?

I again can only sketch a response. First, we remember again that God made us as limited beings and yet dignified our human nature by speaking to the first humans with an expectation that they could understand and respond adequately to him. Not only were Adam and Eve able to know God, but God continued to speak to his people through time and continues to speak to us to this day. We embrace this in faith.

Second, God dignified the lives of Adam and Eve by giving them meaningful work and even allowed Adam to name the animals. They were empowered, in other words, to know the natural world. On a purely secular level, any reasonable person must agree that the arc of the growth of human knowledge, as exemplified by our growing scientific knowledge base and the resulting technological triumphs of the modern age, testifies that fallible as human knowing may be, we have remarkable capacities to know some things truly.

Third, we remember from chapter 2 that seeing truly is not a claim to human perfection or omniscience. We do not have to see anything or everything *perfectly* in order to be gifted to see *rightly enough*. Earlier, I used the illustration of an adequate map that allows us to get from one place to another. In this context, I switch the analogy to that of the walk or the drive itself. As a finite human being, you are incapable of experiencing and processing all the infinite array of possible stimuli that bombard you as you journey from your apartment or dorm to a classroom. You never perceive certain things, and you perceive and forget others, make mistakes such as turning the wrong way at the corner, and so forth. But your human capacities to know, limited as they are, are *sufficient*. You can get from point A to point B. You may not know perfectly, but you know adequately. In the words of missiologist Lesslie Newbigin,[16] our human capacities to know—even to know God's truth—may not generate *perfect certainty*, but they are sufficient for proper human *confidence*. We may not know (or sense or remember) perfectly, but we know (or sense or remember) adequately.

CONCLUSION

The neuroscientific perspectives on human nature can be challenging to Christians. But when we have a proper understanding of humans as biological creatures, though not merely biological creatures, we have the capacity to draw from a rich body of understanding that can inform our understanding of our own humanity.

---

[16] Lesslie Newbigin, *Proper Confidence: Faith, Doubt, and Certainty of Christian Discipleship* (Grand Rapids, MI: Eerdmans, 1995).

4

BEHAVIOR GENETICS AND RESPONSIBLE PERSONHOOD

Jim had been told that he was adopted by his parents, that he was an identical twin, and that his identical twin brother had died in infancy. He grew up doing okay in school in Ohio, loving math and hating spelling, and pursued a job in law enforcement. Jim married Linda, divorced her, and then married his second wife, Betty. He had a son named James Allen and a dog named Toy. His favorite place to go on vacation was Pas Grille Beach in Florida. He smoked Salem cigarettes, chewed his fingernails, and suffered from tension headaches.

Then one day at age thirty-nine, he received a telephone call. The caller identified himself as his identical twin brother, who was not dead after all, but had been adopted into a different family just thirty miles away. The two brothers met for the first time. It was obvious immediately that they looked almost identical. And they quickly discovered that, despite having been raised in different homes with no interaction with each other since their fourth week of life, they had a *lot* in common. Truly.

As incredible as it may sound, my first paragraph describing Jim is accurate for *both* men (Jim Lewis and Jim Springer) with only two exceptions: (1) Jim Springer's adoptive parents had been told that Jim's twin brother was dead, but Jim Lewis's adoptive parents had been told that the other twin was alive; the Lewises told their Jim this fact when he was about age five. (2) The middle name of the oldest son of one of the Jims was spelled *Allen* and the oldest son of the other Jim was spelled *Alan*. Other than that, all the facts above fit both Jims.[1]

Could there be a clearer demonstration of the power of genetics in shaping human personality? Is it all in the genes? Does environment make any difference? Does choice make a difference, and is choice even real? To grapple with these questions, we need to gather some quick background on the nature/nurture debate and on other prominent approaches to the study of human personality.

APPROACHES TO PERSONALITY PSYCHOLOGY

There are many approaches to the scientific study of human personality. An introductory psychology course will look at development, learning, and many other topics. Even in the typical chapter devoted specifically to personality, you will find discussion of a variety of "grand theory" approaches to the study of personality. Your professors will examine such approaches as:

- Psychoanalytic psychology, the approach initiated by Sigmund Freud, who postulated the dominant role of unconscious processes and primitive motivations in the shaping of human behavior, with the more civilized aspects of human personality understood as a veneer over this more primitive base.

- Humanistic psychology, the approach pioneered by Abraham Maslow and Carl Rogers, who emphasized the choices of the human agent and the subjective side of human experience in determining the nature of personhood.

- Trait psychology, dominated today by the "Big 5 Trait" approach to personality summarized by the acronym OCEAN, whereby the majority of the statistical variation in human behavior appears

---

[1] Nancy L. Segal, *Born Together—Reared Apart: The Landmark Minnesota Twins Study* (Cambridge, MA: Harvard University Press, 2012).

to be captured by five inclusive and broad human traits (or variables on which we differ from each other): *openness to experience* (the degree to which one seeks and appreciates new experiences), *conscientiousness* (the degree of organization and persistence we manifest toward self-determined goals), *extroversion/introversion* (the degree to which we are energized by interaction versus preferring a more solitary experience), *agreeableness* (ranging from compassion to antagonism), and *neuroticism* (the degree to which we are prone to emotional agitation and instability).

- Social-cognitive psychology, an approach that emphasizes learning, the critical role of patterns of thinking and perception, and the social context of behavior (including peer groups and culture) on personality, and which assumes a "reciprocal determinism" by which environment influences persons, but persons change their environments with their choices and actions.

The field of personality, at the moment, is abuzz with the examination of genetic contributions to the determination of human behavior. We could focus in a number of directions in thinking about human personality, but consideration of the influence of genetic factors represents special challenges to Christians. At times, such approaches can lead one to feel that human beings are predetermined robots living out scripts set down for us at the moment of conception. To grapple with this from a Christian perspective, we will sketch the nature/nurture problem and then explore behavior genetics.

NATURE VERSUS NURTURE

One of the most persistent debates in psychology has been over whether nature or nurture is dominant in shaping human personality and behavior, with some attempts to balance both factors. Coming into the twentieth century, highly biological explanations enjoyed dominance in the form of theories such as phrenology or the eugenics movement that sought to eradicate physically defective persons and races. In the early twentieth century, the pendulum swung with the rise of the early radical behaviorism that emphasized environmentalism.[2] This suggested that human be-ings—indeed all creatures—were *tabula rasas*, blank slates upon which experience could write without constraint through learning imposed by the environment.

Such environmentalism has fallen on hard times. Doctrinaire behaviorists had assumed that there are no constraints on learning, but a generation ago, an array of animal-learning studies began to suggest otherwise, to suggest that all learning was not the same. The single experiment that exemplifies this trajectory of research demonstrates the remarkable ingenuity of the scientists. And be-cause the results so contradicted environmentalist assumptions, the researchers actually experienced tremendous resistance and dif-ficulty in getting the results published.

This pair of experiments is known together as "The Bright, Noisy, Tasty Water Experiments."[3] The first experiment examined how rats under different learning conditions developed an aversion to flavored water. The experimenters exposed rats to an uncondi-tioned stimulus (US) of mild X-radiation,[4] which has been shown to produce a predictable response of nausea in rats. Just before pre-sentation of this US, they paired it with three kinds of conditioned stimuli (CSs) in four different combinations:

- the first group received the US after exposure to a CS of bright light + loud noise + sweet-tasting water;

- the second group received the US after exposure to a CS of loud noise only + plain-tasting water;

- the third group received the US after exposure to a CS of bright light only + plain tasting water; and

[2] Determination of behavior by the environment; not environmentalism as creation care.
[3] John Garcia and Robert A. Koelling, "Relation of Cue to Consequence in Avoidance Learning," *Psychonomic Science* 4 (1966): 123–24.
[4] Consult your introduction to psychology text for a basic explanation of classical conditioning.

- the fourth group received the US after exposure to a CS of sweet-tasting water only.

Only the first and fourth groups, both involving a sweet taste, developed the predicted aversion to the water. Further, the rats in these groups developed the aversion rapidly, while rats in the second and third conditions failed to develop the aversion despite repeated learning trials. This meant that of the three different conditioned stimuli—light, noise, and sweet taste—only the taste of the water could be associated with the unconditioned stimulus of X-rays that produced nausea. The rats could not learn an association between the unconditioned stimulus that resulted in nausea and either a bright light or a loud noise.

Their second experiment used a painful unconditioned stimulus of shock paired with the same three CSs in the same combinations. The experimenters found that the bright light and loud noise could be associated with the unconditioned stimulus of shock that produced pain, but a sweet taste in the water simply could not be associated with the US.

The conclusion of this study and others like it was that some associations are easier for animals to learn, while others appear to be impossible to learn. These experiments demonstrated rapid, sometimes single-trial acquisition and long-term retention of an association in rats between a distinctive taste (think poisoned or spoiled food) and nausea on the one hand, and a flash of light and/ or loud noise (think fire or lightning) and pain on the other hand. In contrast, no number of forced pairings could ever establish the opposite associations (of a flash of light with nausea or of a distinctive taste with sudden pain).

The explanation offered was that evolution had equipped rats to be quick learners of the pain caused by fire or lightning and of the dangers of eating poisoned or diseased food, which allows them to avoid such events. Studies across various species suggest that species are differentially prepared to learn certain associations and not others, to learn efficiently the right lessons for adaptive advantage. These findings on preparedness for learning, along with other parallel developments in the fields of developmental, behavioral, and cognitive psychology, together indicate that nature sets some parameters on animal and human behavior, learning, personality, and functioning, and further that the kind of environmentalism that would propose complete domination by nurture is simply indefensible.

BEHAVIOR GENETICS

Science changes slowly. It took a long time for experimental findings to convince psychologists once again to pay attention to nature (biological influences on learning and personality). The story of the Jim twins emerged about a decade after the experiment involving rats, at a time when environmental explanations, especially the impact of family on human personality, still exerted dominance. But the story of the Jim twins captivated University of Minnesota psychologist Thomas Bouchard, who within weeks engineered an exhaustive multi-day assessment of the Jim twins and thus launched the *Minnesota Study of Twins Reared Apart* (MISTRA).[5] MISTRA is one of the most influential studies among many major contributions supporting the rise of behavior genetics, the science of studying the role of genetic influences in shaping human behavior.

Over the twenty years following his assessment of the Jim twins, Bouchard's team carefully examined eighty-one monozygotic (one egg)/identical twins *reared apart* and fifty-six dizygotic (two eggs)/fraternal twins reared apart. The twins were compared with each other and with a larger body of monozygotic and dizygotic twins reared together. Siblings, spouses, and others were also assessed for comparative purposes as individuals with less or little genetic relationship. MISTRA gathered huge amounts of data;

---

[5] I draw on the excellent summary of MISTRA by Segal, *Born Together*.

twin pairs were basically kept busy with assessments eight to twelve hours per day for an entire five- to seven-day period, generating thousands of distinct data points on each person.

To understand the power of this research paradigm, it is important to note the role that *experimental control* plays in the advance of scientific understanding. By analogy, it is impossible to do good chemistry on a test tube full of dirt because of the uncertain nature of what you are studying. To do chemistry at all—to understand the behavior of chemical elements—the scientist must refine the focus on a purer substance and eliminate the conflicting effects of extraneous substances and factors that blur the focus of the research. Similarly, in psychology experimenters often struggle to eliminate or control the influence of extraneous factors that might be influencing behavior.

The discovery of identical twins reared apart helped to propel forward the field of behavior genetics. Researchers in this growing field think in terms of three major influences on human behavior and personality: *genetics*, *shared environment*, and *unshared environment*. Shared environment designates those aspects of experience that individuals share in common: children who grow up with the same mother, father, siblings, grandparents, and so forth have common experiences—vacations, meals, tragedy. Unshared environment refers to unique experiences limited to an individual; think of the lucky daughter who gets that loving, creative, extraordinary teacher denied to the other brothers and sisters or the tragically unfortunate daughter abused by an older brother who singled her out in secret.

These are enormous categories, and gaining control on any aspect of the three is a huge step forward. We can estimate the degree to which individuals share their genetic heritage: identical twins share 100 percent of their genes; fraternal twins and regular siblings (brothers and sisters) share genetic similarities limited to the contributions of only two persons (their mother and father);

and adopted children share no more genetic similarity with their adoptive siblings than you find in the general population.

Before the discovery of the Jim twins, researchers could find any number of people who experienced somewhat similar or contrasting shared environments and somewhat similar or contrasting unshared environments, but identical twins reared apart represented for the first time a substantial group of individuals who were *identical genetically* but had experienced almost exclusively unshared environments. This provided new opportunities to pull apart the influence of genes and environment. I will not attempt to explain the statistical science behind it, but this was a huge step forward in estimating the respective power of genetics, shared environment, and unshared environment.

I will focus primarily on the findings of MISTRA as representative of the broad field of behavior genetics. The crude summary is that *it is the rule rather than the exception that there is substantial genetic heritability associated with almost every dimension of human behavior.* Heritability, the primary statistical measure of the percentage of variance accounted for by genetic factors, ranges from zero to one (think of it as 0 percent to 100 percent).

The vast majority of measured psychological traits manifest moderate heritability in the range of .30 to .50. Some psychological characteristics such as intelligence carry a higher genetic heritability, as high as .77, while a few characteristics are less heritable. Traits as diffuse as introversion-extroversion, job satisfaction, one's "happiness set point," ego development, proclivity toward alcoholism or homosexuality, perception of family environment, cognitive processing speed, authoritarianism, and job interests and values all show moderate heritability. Moderate heritability was also found for an array of physical characteristics including proclivity to headaches, weight, risk factors for cardiovascular disease, circadian rhythm, immune response, ophthalmologic refractive error, allergic reactions, age of first menstruation, and vulnerability to periodontal disease.

Findings such as these have produced a remarkable turn of opinion in the field of psychology, a turn toward emphasizing the potency of our genetic heritage in shaping who we are. But it is important to recognize that thoughtful psychologists have offered many qualifications to this emphasis on the influence of genetics, including:

- reminders that the heritability statistic applies only to the particular group studied and is a poor predictor applied to other groups and cannot be used to make estimations regarding individuals;

- recognition that human behavior and personality are much too complex for specific characteristics to be caused by single genes; most likely, multiple genetic tendencies interact in very complex ways;

- development of the new field of epigenetics is grounded in the recognition that many genes are expressed (switched "on") by environmental conditions, thus requiring us to think in terms of complex interactions of genetics and environment.

CHRISTIAN ENGAGEMENT

As the influence of genetics is emphasized, the possibility of human freedom and the influence of our families seem to diminish. What are we to make of this? Has freedom disappeared?[6]

EMBODIMENT AND GENETIC INFLUENCE

As I argued in the last chapter, we begin by embracing embodiment. We are embodied beings; we have limitations, including the limitations imposed by our embodied nature. We may be more than our bodies, but we are bodies. Our genes are the building blocks for everything good about what we are. Our genes establish boundaries and limits to what we can experience and, because of the fall,

---

[6] Parts of the following discussion are drawn from my review for the journal *Books & Culture* of Segal, *Born Together*; and also from an unpublished paper posted on the Web: Stanton L. Jones, "Sexual Orientation and Reason: On the Implications of False Beliefs about Homosexuality," http://www.christianethics.org.

may introduce tendencies that are undesirable (such as neuroticism) or even morally loaded proclivities (such as alcoholism). The experimental findings are compelling: Christians need to be open to the findings that our genes shape our experience.

Christians are particularly prone to resist findings that there are genetic causes to behavior patterns that we consider to be sinful, particularly alcoholism and homosexuality, as mentioned above. Part of this resistance comes from confusion that "genetic cause" equals "genetic determination." Some enthusiasts for the addictions paradigm and some advocates of gay acceptance contribute to this confusion by exaggerating the influence of genetic factors.

A more sober summary of the influence of genetic factors, however, easily shows that these heritability contributions are rarely completely determinative. Huntington's Disease is one of these: if you have the gene for the disease, you *will inevitably develop the disease*. But very few human conditions are like that; most genetic influences are moderate; that is, genetics explains part of the variance in human personality and behavior but leaves much unexplained.

But how are we to understand such moderate levels of causation? One study by a major behavioral geneticist, Robert Plomin,[7] examined the heritability of that most mundane and ubiquitous of behaviors, television watching, and found an average heritability estimate of .45 for the proclivity to watch television, a fairly average level of heritability for most of the psychological and physical variables studied by MISTRA. I have come to think of this finding about proclivity toward television watching as the paradigm through which to understand the issue of human freedom.

We begin by realizing that *meaningful* freedom does not mean *unconstrained* freedom. We are, after all, finite beings; Adam and

---

[7] Robert Plomin et al., "Individual Differences in Television Viewing in Early Childhood: Nature as Well as Nurture," *Psychological Science* 1 (1990): 371–77.

Eve had the freedom to respond appropriately to God's command, but they did not have the freedom to jump to the moon or to become rocks. We should be open to the idea of having proclivities, remembering that our freedom also has been negatively impacted by the fall; unredeemed persons are in bondage to sin, and those who have found faith in Christ are in the process of being released from their bondage to sin as they access the resources of grace.

In dialogue with findings from behavior genetics, we come to a fuller realization that different persons have different kinds and degrees of freedom. The person with a propensity to obesity faces more difficulty making wise food and exercise decisions than the person who does not have the propensity. And genetics is not the only source of propensities; our environment and learning history contribute to propensities as well. The Christian view of persons requires that we have some degree of responsibility in life, but it does not require that we act without influence upon our choice. Precisely how God's providence, our genetic/biological inheritance, our families, our communities, our cultures, and the idiosyncratic events that happen in the course of life interact with the reality of human choice is a great mystery, but one we can celebrate.

Psychologists sometimes speak as if human choice does not exist, but is there actually room for human freedom in the formulations emerging from behavior genetics? Despite not having final answers for this enormously complex problem, I continue to believe that freedom—defined as the capacity to exercise meaningful choice even as we are influenced by other variables—exists for the following reasons.

First, we are active in shaping what we experience. Eric Turkheimer argues that the small, measured effect of shared environment may be partially attributable to what he calls the "effective environment."[8] In short, he challenges the idea of shared environ-

---

[8] Eric Turkheimer, "Three Laws of Behavior Genetics and What They Mean," *Current Directions in Psychological Science* 9 (2000): 162.

ment as two people actually experiencing and being influenced by the same environment. Do a first child and youngest child really have the same family environment? Not only does one have a younger sibling and the other an older sibling (which is different), but they also experience a somewhat similar environment in different ways, as when the introverted child experiences an interaction with a parent differently than an extroverted child. The effective environment is *the environment as subjectively experienced by the child*. No two children ever experience the exact same parenting or familial environment, because they think of it and respond to it differently. Perhaps one way that we exercise choice is in the attitudes we adopt to process what we experience as we participate in creating our own effective environments.

Second, there are actually four, not three, categories in the statistical equation measuring heritability: genes, shared environment, unshared environment, *and error variance*. This last category is assumed by psychologists to be "statistical noise," the result of the limitations of our methodologies. But might there be more in the category of error variance than just error variance? If this category contains the statistical measures of variations in behavior that the statistical models cannot predict, wouldn't this be where meaningful human choice would show up? We would expect there to be error variance if individuals were actually making somewhat unpredictable decisions because they act as free agents at times. An example might be the individual powerfully predisposed toward alcoholism by genetic inheritance, by family exposure to alcoholic parental modeling, and by prior experience as a young adult, but who nevertheless makes the surprising decision to pursue treatment and live sober. This person's statistical profile might predict a life of addiction, but the presence of error variance is the mathematical acknowledgment that people don't always behave as the formulas predict. There is room, statistically, for some level of human freedom.

We can bring these threads together by thinking of that one area of our lives where we most fundamentally understand ourselves as free: what we choose to believe in terms of religious faith. It may distress some to know that MISTRA and other behavior genetics studies have found that religiousness is moderately to strongly heritable (about .50). In response, we must understand that religiousness is a measure of the style or degree of passion with which people tend to approach their experience of religious faith; it does not indicate determination of specific religious beliefs. Segal recounts the stories of two identical twin sets raised apart under very different religions, and each set of twins were, in accord with their adoptive family tradition, respectively Jewish and Catholic.[9] These twins were moderately similar in the *style* with which they approach their religiousness but adopted *different faiths*. Neither they nor we are religiously preprogrammed.

DO FAMILIES MATTER?

Christians emphasize that families matter in the shaping of children. This in part comes from the instruction of Scripture, such as the many injunctions in the book of Proverbs for children to obey their parents and parents to discipline well their children. Communities, of course, are also charged to reinforce such commitments and assist in the training of children.

But why bother if parents have little influence? It is common today for estimates of parental influence to be extremely modest. This can be illustrated by a quote from a popular introduction to psychology textbook in which, in response to the question, "To what extent are our lives shaped by early stimulation, by parents, and by peers?," the author states:

> Parents influence their children in areas such as manners and political and religious beliefs, but not in other areas, such as

[9] Segal, *Born Together*, 46, 145.

84 **PSYCHOLOGY**

personality. Language and other behaviors are shaped by peer
groups, as children adjust to fit in. By choosing their children's
neighborhoods and schools, parents can exert some influence
over peer group culture.[10]

The implication seems to be that genes do the heavy lifting, the
peer group does most of the rest, and family contributes a little
guidance over peer group but nothing more. Similarly, Segal states,
"environmental effects that are most important in personality development appear to be those that are experienced apart from the
family—the nonshared environmental factors." These are remark-
ably modest estimates of the possible influence of parents over
their children. But is there more to this than we think?

Turkheimer's idea of effective environment is again helpful here. In reality, no two children are impacted the same way
by parenting, and this complicates the measurement of parental
influence. Simplistically, do any two children ever experience the
same family, school, or culture? Imagine a dinner conversation in a
nuclear family of four in which one child is happy because of a loving interaction with one parent right before dinner, while the other
child is sullen and withdrawn because of a punitive interaction
with the other parent. Is this a *shared* environment? Or do the two
children have different experiences of the same empirical reality?

Turkheimer concludes that the consistent, empirical findings
that shared environmental influences exert little power is probably
an illusion driven by the methodologies by which we measure heritability; these methodologies fail to reflect how individual children
in the same family and culture experience differently the shared
family and culture. He concludes that "the apparent victory of
nature over nurture . . . is thus seen to be more methodological than
substantive. We need not conclude that aspects of families children
share with siblings are of no causal importance."[11]

---

[10] David G. Myers, *Psychology*, 9th ed. (New York: Worth, 2010), 170.
[11] Turkheimer, "Three Laws," 162–63.

And Turkheimer has produced empirical data contributing, in my mind, to these discussions about freedom. Turkheimer studies intelligence and academic performance. Despite strong findings of genetic heritability for intelligence that parallel that of MISTRA, he still champions the important role of environment. Why? Because heritability estimates shift in light of other pressures.[12] Specifically, Turkheimer and his colleagues have found that heritability estimates for intelligence *differ between the rich and the poor.*

Environment appears to matter little among the rich because those of us who are advantaged can provide sufficient environmental supports—music lessons, books, educational puzzles, and toys for children to advance their intellectual development—such that the heights that the children reach are determined almost entirely by their genetic range. For the rich, environment maxes out, so to speak, leaving only heritability to determine achievement.

Poor children, in contrast, respond much more powerfully to the environment. On the one hand, a poor child with no educational opportunities is cheated due to lack of resources in actualizing the genetic potentialities she might have for intellectual achievement. On the other hand, the poor child who is blessed with that determined parent, or given that scholarship grant to go to a charter school, or who happens to be in a neighborhood with an effective Head Start program, might capitalize on every God-given cognitive synapse. For the poor, small differences in environment can have huge impact on the maximization of the potential granted from heritability.

So parents may indeed have a powerful impact, being that potent environmental force that can make a difference in a child's life. Part of being this kind of influential parent requires effectively matching your parenting style to the needs of your children, particularly according to their character and personality. Segal picks

---

[12] E. Turkheimer, A. Haley, B. D'Onofrio, M. Waldron, and I. I. Gottesman, "Socioeconomic Status Modifies Heritability of IQ in Young Children," *Psychological Science* 14 (2003): 623–28.

up on this, saying, "One implication of our work was that parents should pay close attention to each child's unique character traits and nurture each child's individual interests. Paradoxically, parental fairness seems more likely to come from treating children differently in accordance with their individual behaviors than from treating them alike."[13]

CONCLUSION

In chapter 2 I argued that as Christians we assume freedom as a fundamental part of what it means to be human. The strong findings for the influence of genetics in shaping personality seem to run counter to this assumption. But by interacting with the findings of behavior genetics in the shaping of personality, we can begin to appreciate the way that our embodiment shapes the contours of who we are as persons yet without robbing us of the possibility of meaningful choice. Our parents have a powerful if limited influence on who we become. Similarly, our choices have limited but meaningful implications for our lives. We may not be able to choose anything we might want, but we can choose some things.

---

[13] Segal, *Born Together*, 102.

5

POSITIVE AND APPLIED PSYCHOLOGY AND SANCTIFICATION

A great deal of my professional attention has been devoted to Christian appraisal of the applied fields of clinical, counseling, and other therapeutic forms of psychology.[1] Appropriation of psychotherapy and counseling tools by Christians, even if performed by Christian professionals, has been the subject of criticism by proponents of Christian counseling who are zealous to protect the church from the encroachment of secular philosophies and practices.

Such critics have argued that the work of integration, of bringing sacred and secular perspectives into dialogue, is intrinsically demeaning to the Scriptures as the Word of God. We have already addressed such criticisms implicitly in chapters 1 and 2. But other arguments have been raised specifically to the adoption of *applied* psychological methods by Christians. Briefly:

1) It is sin that afflicts human beings and leads to psychological suffering. Secular psychological interventions necessarily deal only with superficial aspects of the person, and in the process of attempting to produce happiness and better adjustment via human effort, such methods undermine the work of

---

[1] In this chapter I will be drawing extensively from such works as Stanton L. Jones and Richard E. Butman, *Modern Psychotherapies: A Comprehensive Christian Appraisal*, 2nd ed. (Downers Grove, IL: InterVarsity, 2012); and Stanton L. Jones, "An Apologetic Apologia for the Integration of Psychology and Theology," in *The Care for the Soul: Exploring the Intersection of Psychology and Theology*, ed. T. R. Phillips and M. R. McMinn (Downers Grove, IL: InterVarsity, 2001), 62–77.

the Holy Spirit in convicting the lost sinner of the need for salvation.

2) God's intended work in the life of the believer is sanctification. Scripture teaches that the efforts of the flesh—unaided human effort as exemplified in applied psychology—can contribute nothing to this process.

3) The Christian church is the intended locus of God's work of healing, blessing, and grace in the lives of broken sinners, who obtain healing through the blood and work of Christ. The practice of psychotherapy apart from the church undermines the witness of the church as Christ's body.

These are complex arguments. I will provide here a brief sketch of responses and then move to more in-depth Christian reflection on one current, influential manifestation of applied psychology—the positive psychology movement.

First, the critic is correct that sin is our most basic affliction, but this argument fails to take into a full account the complex nature of sin. As discussed earlier, sin is rebellion, disbelief, and disobedience, but it is also at least two additional things: brokenness, and an external force pressing against us to push us away from God. It is sin as brokenness that provides an entrée for the use of applied psychology. First Thessalonians 5:14 provides guidance for ministry: "We urge you, brothers, admonish the idle, encourage the fainthearted, help the weak, be patient with them all." These are not exhaustive instructions, but they suggest some helpful categories to use in our analysis. The word "idle" in that verse literally means undisciplined or insubordinate and seems to refer to those who are deliberately sinning, and to these we are counseled to provide exhortation or correction.

But that is not the only need. Those who are discouraged need to be filled with encouragement, and those who are weak need to be strengthened or helped. Those who struggle with psychological disorders certainly do struggle with some deliberate sins but can more be characterized as the fainthearted and the weak, those characterized by a lack of strength, inspiration, skill, resources, or force of will. They do not need to be browbeaten about their sin but rather need tangible help.

There is a great deal of scientific evidence about the effectiveness of a variety of secular approaches to psychotherapy interventions and a growing body of evidence regarding the effectiveness of approaches to counseling that are specifically tailored for Christian populations.[2] Psychological approaches can help people who are depressed, anxious, experiencing relational conflict, and the like, and in the absence of a strong justification for withholding the kind of help that tangible, empirically validated approaches offer to such persons, Christian compassion should incline us toward helping them.

At one level, helping a suicidally depressed individual to achieve a more even keel can be seen justifiably as superficial. After all, that person may feel better after intervention but be no closer to eternal life with God. And while it might be that God is using depression to break down one's defenses and draw him closer to the embrace of Christ's love, it is the experience of many that depression or another difficulty prevents them from seeing the love of God or of dealing directly with spiritual questions of eternal significance. Sometimes, tangible help can contribute to clearing away the fog so that the person can turn to deeper matters. Further, it is possible that such persons will experience the love of God *through* a tangible extension of help. The Christian practitioner delivering such care to an unbeliever can remind him, as so many do, that resolution of concrete suffering is only the first step in the kind of healing that the loving Father God wants to offer each of us.

Second, the criticism that the efforts of the flesh can never

---

[2] Everett Worthington Jr., Eric L. Johnson, Joshua Hook, and Jamie D. Aten, *Evidence-Based Practices for Christian Counseling and Psychotherapy* (Downers Grove, IL: InterVarsity, 2013).

really help in the task of sanctification suffers from confusion about the nature of the flesh. In the New Testament, the term *flesh* refers to the sinful nature, not simply to human effort. Indeed, Scripture often urges us to deeper and more stringent efforts, to strive with all our might toward holiness. The apostles urge us to "put on the new self" and to "put off [the] old self" (Eph. 4:22–24) and to "cleanse ourselves from every defilement of body and spirit" (2 Cor. 7:1); they offer constant exhortation toward human effort even as we depend upon God's grace. Yes, improvement in some psychological dysfunction is not the same thing as sanctification (which is growth in godliness), but it can be a building block on which positive movement can be built.

Third, the church is indeed God's intended context for healing.[3] It is indeed a problem that so many churches have given up on the ministry of healing, in part because they have shifted that responsibility onto the secular mental-health professions. Churches need to recapture their confidence that the answers to life's problems are found in the Scriptures, in the Holy Spirit as the divine healer, and in God's heart to provide meaningful growth and healing in the process of sanctification. But just as we have made room for the practice of medicine as an instrument of healing, so also there may be room for Christians to adopt worthwhile practices from the secular mental-health fields to concretely help those who are suffering.

These methods should not be adopted uncritically. In the introduction, I spoke briefly of the critical and then the constructive phases of the work of integration. Before one moves to adopt concepts and practices from a secular field, one should first think critically about those concepts and practices from a Christian perspective. Once we have thought critically, it would seem wise to appropriate that which is good in an attempt to move constructively in one's engagement with truth.

---

[3] Jones, "An Apologetic Apologia."

My coauthors and I adopted just this strategy of critically evaluating and constructively appropriating aspects of the various secular approaches to psychotherapy in our book *Modern Psychotherapies: A Comprehensive Christian Appraisal*.[4] We examined each approach from a Christian perspective, including its philosophical assumptions, basic model of human personality, hypotheses about the nature of abnormality, model of what it means to be healthy, methods by which it proposes to induce change, and evidence regarding its effectiveness.

That book can be consulted for Christian appraisals of the four dominant approaches to human change today—psychodynamic therapy, cognitive therapy, experiential therapy, and family therapy—as well as quite a number of other approaches to change. In this chapter I will apply the same basic, analytical approach to a newer, burgeoning approach to applied psychology.

POSITIVE PSYCHOLOGY

The positive psychology (PP) movement is a fascinating development in the field. Though it is not often treated as a separate subject in an introductory psychology course, it is garnering an extraordinary amount of attention in the public media. Popular books on the topic appear on bookshelves. In the business world, workshops, seminars, and training programs utilize the tools and approaches of PP. Perhaps most significantly, elementary- and secondary-school curricula are beginning to offer instruction in PP as a scientific approach to the pursuit of happiness and well-being.

There is a narrative that drives the PP movement: throughout its early history, psychology was a purely academic discipline. A good deal of the interest of scholars in the field was on optimal, positive human functioning. For instance, intelligence researchers were as interested (or more) in giftedness and genius as they were in intellectual dysfunction; personality researchers were just as inter-

---

[4] Jones and Butman, *Modern Psychotherapies*.

ested in positive attributes as negative and dysfunctional attributes. But as psychology began to be used as a tool in military screening to weed out those unfit to serve, its focus began to move toward preoccupation with dysfunction.

This move intensified as psychology was incorporated into the Veteran Administration's rehabilitation efforts for veterans of World War II and after. Following the money trail, psychology was increasingly less of an academic discipline and more of a professional guild, part of a medical care system that has always been driven by treatment of disease and pathology instead of strategies for the promotion of health. Psychologists could get remuneration for treating disorders; there was little money in optimizing human functioning. The field became preoccupied with disease, pathology, and disorder, largely at the individual level.

Positive psychology aims to change all that. One author defines PP as "concerned with the use of psychological theory, research, and intervention techniques to understand [and enhance] the positive, adaptive, creative, and emotionally fulfilling aspects of human behavior";[5] and another as:

> the scientific study of optimal human functioning. At the meta-psychological level, it aims to redress the imbalance in psychological research and practice by calling attention to the positive aspects of human functioning and experience, and integrating them with our understanding of the negative aspects of human functioning and experience. At the pragmatic level, it is about understanding the *wellsprings*, *processes* and *mechanisms* that lead to desirable *outcomes*.[6]

The scope of attention of this new field is extraordinarily broad. Martin Seligman, widely credited as officially founding the field of

---

[5] William Compton and Edward Hoffman, *Positive Psychology: The Science of Happiness and Flourishing* (Belmont, CA: Wadsworth, 2013), 1.
[6] P. Alex Linley et al., "Positive Psychology: Past, Present and (Possible) Future," *Journal of Positive Psychology* 1 (2006): 8, emphasis original.

positive psychology during his term as president of the American Psychological Association, describes three levels of focus of PP:

> The field of positive psychology at the subjective level [also called "positive experience"] is about valued subjective experiences: well-being, contentment, and satisfaction (in the past); hope and optimism (for the future); and flow and happiness (in the present). At the individual level [also called "positive personality"] it is about positive individual traits: the capacity for love and vocation, courage, interpersonal skill. . . . At the group level [also called "positive communities and institutions"], it is about the civic virtues and institutions that move individuals towards better citizenship: responsibility, nurturance, altruism, civility.[7]

THE PHILOSOPHY OF POSITIVE PSYCHOLOGY

PP proponent Alan Waterman asked why advocates for PP and representatives of humanistic psychology, an older tradition in the field that has also focused on positive attributes, have not collaborated more. He states that "the tension between these two perspectives is a function of the extensive differences in their philosophical grounding. Because proponents of humanistic and positive psychology *start with different premises about human nature and the nature of the psychological enterprise*, it has proven very difficult for them to identify common ground, even when the objectives they pursue appear similar."[8]

Waterman concludes that the two subfields differ with respect to their *ontology* or fundamental perspectives on the nature of the reality being studied, their *epistemology* or understanding of how best to examine and study the phenomena of interest, and their *practical philosophy* or ethical reasoning by which value is ascribed

---

[7] Martin Seligman and Mihaly Csikszentmihalyi, "Positive Psychology: An Introduction," *American Psychologist*, 55 (2000): 5.

[8] Alan Waterman, "The Humanistic Psychology—Positive Psychology Divide," *American Psychologist* 68 (2013): 124, emphasis added. Waterman's analysis can in many ways serve as a model for how Christians should engage every aspect of the entire field; though he does not utilize a Christian perspective, he asks deep, broad questions precisely as a thoughtful religious believer should.

to different characteristics, goals, or outcomes that are pursued. Waterman concludes that the emerging field of PP is characterized by the following:

- *Ontology*. In contrast to a humanistic belief that human will can determine the totality of one's being, for "positive psychologists, there is not only a generic human nature but also an individual nature."[9] There are fundamental givens about humans in general, but individual persons are not all the same. Some have to fight harder than others to develop positive character traits that foster happiness and well-being.

- *Epistemology*. In contrast to a humanistic preoccupation with subjective experience, positive psychologists embrace traditional methods of science and the use of qualitative methodologies with rigorous experimental and statistical controls with a strong degree of confidence that they will produce useful information.

- *Practical philosophy*. Humanistic approaches emphasize choices of the self and understanding of one's phenomenological experience in the moment, but interventions rarely are goal-directed toward specific positive outcomes. In contrast, PP is highly pragmatic, "directing the client's attention to what can be done now to make incremental improvements in quality of life. The aim is to start a virtuous cycle whereby immediate improvements in mood, character strength, or problem-solving leads to greater optimism that further improvements are possible in the future. The techniques used are generally short-term and exercise oriented."[10]

A brief interaction with Waterman's summary from our commitments to Christian truth can help us get our bearings.

ONTOLOGY

Christians would certainly agree with the characterization of PP that there is such a thing as generic human nature and specific in-

---

[9] Ibid., 127.
[10] Ibid., 129.

dividual natures. Human character is not undefined, a blank slate, subject without limit to the will of the human agent. Like proponents of PP, we affirm that we nevertheless are not helpless robots predetermined by our biological and environmental heritage. We have responsible if limited freedom.

But Christians must contest some of the specific hypotheses of PP. Seligman has argued that the Christian doctrine of original sin is to blame for the negative focus of psychology: "This 'rotten-to-the-core' view pervades Western thought, and if there is any doctrine positive psychology seeks to overthrow it is this one. Its original manifestation is the doctrine of original sin."[11] His core objection is to the attribution that all *positive* traits and motivations—as understood in Christian theology and in various forms of negative psychology such as psychoanalysis—ultimately devolve to be understood as secondary to the more fundamental negative traits and motivations. His suggested alternative? "More plausible is the dual aspect theory that the strengths and the virtues are just as basic to human nature as the negative traits."[12] The transcendent standard by which we judge traits to be positive/virtuous or negative is unaddressed.

Properly understood, Christian theological anthropology is not the source of the negative focus of psychology and in reality is *more* positive than PP. The "dual aspect theory" proposed by Seligman treats the good and the bad of human nature as "just as basic"; the Christian view is much more positive: human beings were first created perfect and in the image of God. We were, in God's words, "very good." Sin postdates the perfect goodness of creation and thus represents a corruption of what was originally good. Sin contaminates the good, but because each member of the human race is made in the image of God, that which is good in us cannot be obliterated. As discussed in chapter 2, original sin is the doctrine that all of us are sinful from birth; there is no pure inno-

[11] Martin Seligman, "Positive Psychology: Fundamental Assumptions," *The Psychologist* 16 (2003): 126. Many humanistic psychologists have argued the same.
[12] Ibid., 127.

cence in human experience. The doctrine of total depravity does not mean we are totally evil; it means instead that every aspect of our experience is tainted or contaminated to some degree by sin. Total depravity does not deny what is good about us. Thus, the goodness of humanity is more fundamental, more basic, than sin.

EPISTEMOLOGY

Christian theology and the Christian intellectual tradition provide a strong foundation for scientific inquiry. We can celebrate, with positive psychologists, the value of scientific study. But we are not limited to scientific study. We also value pure reason and other faculties by which humanity pursues truth, including the faculties of artistic expression such as poetry and music.[13]

One of the challenges of the PP movement is the relationship of science and values. In some publications, PP proponents speak as if they are attempting to do value-free science in true Enlightenment style. Seligman claims to be developing a "terminology upon which a scientifically viable positive psychology might rest."[14] He divides positive emotions into two categories: pleasures and gratifications. The pleasures include more primitive bodily pleasures (the taste of sugar, the pleasure of sexual stimulation) and the higher pleasures (the joy of laughter, the fun of play). The gratifications are activities that we enjoy and the outcomes those pursuits create, particularly "*flow*, a state in which time stops and one feels completely at home. The gratifications cannot be obtained or permanently increased without developing the *strengths* and *virtues*."[15]

On this basis, he proposes a three-part terminology that can serve as a foundation for a "scientifically viable positive psychology"[16]: the pursuit of the pleasant life, the good life, and

---

[13] See Jeffrey C. Davis and Philip G. Ryken, *Liberal Arts for the Christian Life* (Wheaton, IL: Crossway, 2012).

[14] Seligman, "Positive Psychology: Fundamental Assumptions," 127.

[15] Ibid., 127, emphases original.

[16] Ibid.

the meaningful life. The pleasant life is one characterized by the pleasures. The good life is one characterized by the gratifications. The meaningful life "adds one more component to the good life—*it is the use of your strengths and virtues in the service of something much larger than you are.*"[17]

Clearly, PP does not fit the mold of value-free, purely objective science, with its talk of pleasures and gratifications, strengths and virtues, the pleasant life, the good life, and the meaningful life. PP is a clear example of what theologian Don Browning has asserted, that psychological science (and particularly the applied psychologies) "cannot avoid a metaphysical and ethical horizon."[18] Psychology is pervaded with ethics and issues of value, as is clearly in evidence in PP. Indeed, in one of the original pronouncements of the contours of PP, one of its cofounders stated, "I [Csikszentmihalyi] was looking for a scientific approach to human behavior, but I never dreamed that this would yield a value-free understanding."[19]

When it is clear that science is explicitly incorporating values, we must carefully evaluate the value claims by biblical standards. We will do this in the balance of this chapter.

PRACTICAL PHILOSOPHY

The pragmatism of PP is both a strength and a weakness. It is taken as a given that human beings are and should be about the pursuit of happiness and personal well-being. At one level, there is an intuitive truthfulness to this claim. But, on the other hand, the Christian faces complications in pursuing happiness and well-being. We cannot evade the reality that PP grounds its approach to the pursuit of virtue and happiness on the fact that it is good for oneself. This is at odds with Christian views of sanctification, of pursuing self-transformation for the glory of God, not the happiness of self.

---

[17] Ibid., emphasis original.

[18] Don Browning and Terry Cooper, *Religious Thought and the Modern Psychologies*, 2nd ed. (Minneapolis: Fortress, 2004), xiv.

[19] Csikszentmihalyi, in "Positive Psychology: Fundamental Assumptions," 7.

But, paradoxically, as Christ exhorts us to sacrifice everything for the sake of the kingdom, and in making that sacrifice, in losing everything, we will gain everything. "What does it profit a man to gain the whole world and forfeit his soul?" asks the Lord Jesus in Mark 8:36. Yet in forfeiting our soul, we learn from our Lord that he "came that they may have life and have it abundantly" (John 10:10). Further, the pursuit of holiness is of such high priority that Christ instructs us to consider enormous sacrifice—the loss of a hand or an eye—for its sake. And yet the reward of holiness is a glorious and everlasting life.

POSITIVE PSYCHOLOGY IN PRACTICE

The field of positive psychology is new and evolving quickly. It seeks to promote happiness, high quality of life, and a general sense of well-being. Positive emotions, actions, and traits are seen as having the power to ameliorate and prevent much of what we experience as severe maladjustment. Seligman has articulated the goals for individual positive psychology psychotherapy (PPP) in terms of six master virtues, each of which is characterized by one of twenty-four specific character strengths, summarized in the table below:[20]

Master Virtues and Associated Character Strengths of Positive Psychology

Virtues	Character Strengths
Wisdom and knowledge	Creativity, curiosity, open-mindedness, love of learning, perspective
Courage	Authenticity, bravery, persistence, zest
Humanity	Kindness, love, social intelligence
Justice	Fairness, leadership, teamwork
Temperance	Forgiveness, modesty, prudence, self-regulation
Transcendence	Appreciation of beauty and excellence, gratitude, hope, humor, religiousness

[20] Martin Seligman et al., "Positive Psychology Progress: Empirical Validation of Interventions," *American Psychologist* 60 (2005): 412.

How do positive psychologists attempt to develop such virtues and strengths? Psychotherapy in this tradition is strongly oriented toward structured exercises that produce immediate, tangible, and concrete movement toward enhanced well-being and happiness, teaching skills that produce such immediate results. Examples of such exercises include the following:[21]

- Identifying signature strengths: direct instruction in virtues and character strengths, with self-assessment and assignments to illustrate and exercise one's signature strengths;

- Good versus bad memories: exploration of expression of negative emotion related to bad memories and emphasis on the cultivation of recollecting good memories;

- Forgiveness: introduction of forgiveness as a practice that can transform anger and bitterness into positive emotions to the benefit of the person who forgives;

- Gratitude: cultivation of client gratitude as a way of maintaining positive focus;

- Optimism and hope: fostering of client memories of former positive resolutions of difficult experiences and identification of positive outcomes;

- Savoring: deliberate cultivation of distinct awareness of pleasure and a disciplined pursuit of pleasurable activities.

In perhaps one of the more remarkable empirical findings of PP, Seligman found positive outcomes with clinically depressed individuals who experienced an Internet-based educational program with very little direct therapeutic involvement.[22] Such a cost-effective and easily disseminated method—if treatment effectiveness

---

[21] From Martin Seligman et al., "Positive Psychotherapy," *American Psychologist* 61 (2006): 782–83.
[22] Seligman et al., "Positive Psychology Progress."

was replicated and further validated—would be a significant addition to the treatment literature.

Positive psychologists, seeing the broad potential applicability of their methods beyond therapy, have moved aggressively into the practice of prevention of dysfunction by the proactive building of positive strengths on a broad basis. One example of positive prevention work is the implementation in school settings of the *Strengths Gym,* a multiyear intervention for adolescents aged twelve to fourteen. Whereas the exercises above were implemented with clients experiencing clinical levels of distress and dysfunction, the *Strengths Gym* is an exercise of "primary prevention," the teaching of psychological principles and methods to a broad population *not* identified as dysfunctional in the hope of preventing future distress.

Students receiving the *Strengths Gym* intervention package learned the same sort of exercises as noted above, with the goal of building future capacity for happiness and well-being as well as resilience against distress. They were trained to identify an array of possible strengths, to build on their existing strengths, and also to learn new strengths and to recognize and affirm the strengths of others. The educators used the *Values in Action* framework, "a comprehensive classification and measurement system"[23] of the virtues and character strengths summarized in the table above. In this study, as in others that have studied positive psychotherapy and prevention, strong positive results were demonstrated from the interventions.

CHRISTIAN CRITIQUE OF POSITIVE PSYCHOLOGY

Christian psychologists have begun to offer constructive criticisms of PP. One of the first was Larry Crabb: "First, let's welcome the focus on joy. Second, let's insist that real joy can never be manufac-

[23] Carmel Proctor et al., "Strengths Gym: The Impact of Character Strengths-Based Intervention on the Life Satisfaction and Well-Being of Adolescents," *Journal of Positive Psychology* 6 (2011): 378.

tured. But counterfeit joy can. And counterfeit joy can become our obsession and keep us from the real thing. The real deal flows out of worship, out of valuing God more than anyone or anything else, even more than the experience of happiness. And the prelude to worship is brokenness, then repentance, then surrender."[24] Siang-Yang Tan offers very similar perspectives.[25]

Thus the question is raised, is PP grounded in selfishness? As mentioned above, even in asking us to sacrifice everything, Christ promises us abundant and eternal life. In challenging us to love others sacrificially, he urges us to do unto others as unto ourselves. He does not ignore our self-interest. But in PP, there appears to be nothing beyond self-interest, at least nothing transcendent. This is problematic.

Theologian Ellen Charry offered insights suggesting that Protestant emphases on sinful human nature can lead us to understand holiness merely as the purging of negative, sinful traits. But holiness is not merely the absence of sin; it is something positive, a trajectory of growth in Christ into union with God. She notes that the Spirit grafts us into the death of Christ but also into the resurrection and ascension of the risen Christ, who toils at the right hand of the Father (Eph. 2:1–10). With the rejuvenating power of the Spirit assisting us, we are able to dwell in the Son and, by his association with the Father, in the very fullness of the triune God, as suggested by John 15:3–11.[26] This is a helpful reminder to Christians that the virtues are something positive to pursue both in life and in science.

But now we turn our attention to perhaps the most important point to make in analyzing PP: the reality that all human understandings of virtues are specific to the particular frameworks or

[24] Larry Crabb, "Positive Psychology: More Narcissism? Or a Welcome Corrective?," *Christian Counseling Today* 12 (2004): 64.
[25] Siang-Yang Tan, "Applied Positive Psychology: Putting Positive Psychology into Practice," *Journal of Psychology and Christianity* 25 (2006): 72.
[26] Ellen Charry, "Positive Theology: An Exploration in Theological Psychology and Positive Psychology," *Journal of Psychology and Christianity* 30 (2011): 292.

systems of belief in which they are grounded.[27] For instance, courage that is grounded in fatalism or hopelessness is not the same thing as courage grounded in trust of God. Pagan hope is not the same thing as Christian hope; pagan gratitude is not the same thing as Christian gratitude. Such virtues, complex as they are, take unique form and shape in the broader context of Christian belief. The Christian virtues have their full and distinct meaning only in the broad context of the total structure of Christian belief and practice.

So what is the framework or system of beliefs from which the virtues of PP are defined? The definitive account of how a consensual group of virtues was developed for PP is illuminating. "Our initial brainstorming about positive characteristics spontaneously took place at the level of character strengths." Panels of experts weeded out redundancies and grouped similar strengths conceptually. A final list emerged, along with a list of ten "criteria for a Strength of Character." These "criteria were articulated after we had identified many dozens of candidate strengths and needed a way to consolidate them. We came up with these 10 criteria by scrutinizing the candidate strengths and looking for common features."[28]

One normally thinks of criteria as the rules by which items are selected, but this method reveals the circularity of the process: the candidate strengths were selected according to unknown criteria, and then the ten criteria were generated to justify the list of candidate strengths! As the PP virtues are elaborated and science is invoked, there is much allusion to "consensus" that this virtue or that practice is universally esteemed or self-evidently understood as good. But it is in their chapter, "Universal Virtues? Lessons from

---

[27] For a sophisticated development of this idea, see Robert C. Roberts, "Studying Virtues," in *Emotions in the Moral Life* (New York: Cambridge University Press, 2013), chap. 1; as well as Robert C. Roberts and W. Jay Wood, *Intellectual Virtues: An Essay in Regulative Epistemology* (New York: Oxford University Press, 2007).

[28] Christopher Peterson and Martin Seligman, *Character Strengths and Virtues: A Handbook and Classification* (Washington, DC: American Psychological Association, 2004), 15–17.

History" that some of the sources of the values infusing the PP movement are suggested.[29]

The authors argue that the list of virtues and character strengths of the PP movement are essentially universally acclaimed and accepted. In tracing the six fundamental virtues across the arc of world culture, other great traditions—Confucianism, Buddhism, Hinduism, classical Greek philosophies, Judaism, Islam— are all given careful consideration. However, their treatment of Christianity is another story.[30] The New Testament is ignored in its entirety, as is the great tradition of Eastern Orthodoxy and Protestantism. Roman Catholicism and essentially all of Christianity is summarized with a cursory treatment of the virtues according to Thomas Aquinas, whose work is treated as a footnote to Aristotle's understanding of virtues. This is a surprising sidelining of the deep tradition of Christian reflection on the virtues that have been so pivotal in the formation of Western civilization. It even risks misunderstanding the work of Aquinas, who did not slavishly follow Aristotle but rather transformed the work of Aristotle in light of Christian commitments.

It comes as no surprise, then, that the virtues as articulated by secular PP and the virtues as understood within Christian faith do not quite line up. If we strive to follow in the steps of Aquinas in adhering to distinctively Christian understandings of the virtues, what might be the result? One Christian psychologist has provided a helpful first approach to this challenge. Fraser Watts and his colleagues raised profound points about some of the specific virtues promoted by PP, specifically:[31]

- *Forgiveness.* Forgiveness in PP is often presented in a rather superficial, therapeutic context as a practice for making one happy. Watts notes that "therapeutic forgiveness [as promoted by PP] as-

[29] Ibid., 33–52.
[30] Ibid., 47–48.
[31] Fraser Watts et al., "Human Spiritual Qualities: Integrating Psychology and Religion," *Mental Health, Religion and Culture* 9 (2006): 277–89.

sumes that forgiveness originates with the victim, whereas religious thinking often assumes that forgiveness originates with God, and that victims who forgive are participating in something bigger than themselves. That is an attributional difference with quite far-reaching psychological implications." Indeed. Forgiveness for PP is primarily about feeling better, whereas forgiveness in Christian perspective can be profoundly sacrificial. Further, "psychology is almost entirely concerned with giving forgiveness, whereas religion is concerned in a more balanced way with both receiving and giving it."[32]

- *Gratitude.* Watts notes that gratitude is usually extended to another person who has made a conscious effort to do something kind or helpful to the recipient. Gratitude for a gift from another human being is understandable, but how does one understand an unbeliever's gratitude for a beautiful day, or for that person's positive traits and gifts, or for life itself? There is something confused about being grateful to a meaningless universe of the benefits that have come one's way. Further, Christian faith calls us to thankfulness at all times for whatever God gives, not only when what is given makes us happy.

- *Hope.* Watts describes the differing ways of conceptualizing hope in secular and religious terms. On the one hand, "psychological research on the implications of hopefulness for mental-health seem largely to have been measuring optimism," a belief that good outcomes are going to accrue to that person. On the other hand, "religious hope is essentially hoping *in* God, not just hoping that certain outcomes will occur."[33] Religious hope is more connected with the wishes and desires of God than with simply wishing that positive outcomes would come one's way.

There is much more work to be done in articulating distinctively Christian understandings of the virtues and of character strengths.[34] Following on these efforts, there is even more work to

---

[33] Ibid., 286–287.
[34] See Roberts and Wood, *Intellectual Virtues*, for a sophisticated guide to getting started.

be done in understanding how to best foster the development of virtues and character strengths, and we can do so with some confidence that these often will foster happiness and well-being. But we should be careful to apply the various methods and practices of PP with a constructively critical eye, ensuring that the virtues and interventions of interest are consistent with biblical understanding of human needs.

CONCLUSION

Perhaps in the enthusiasm for positive psychology we are seeing the phenomenon noted earlier by an esteemed neuroscientist, that "there is a sense that what is most important and distinctly human has slipped through the fingers of the grasp of science. Somehow the new conceptions of human nature fall short of coherence with the fullness of life as actually lived and experienced. They fail to sustain our sense of irreducible personal identity, our capacity for free choice, and our commitment to ideals and transcendent truths."[35] In the presence of such a vacuum, positive psychology seems to be confidently, if naïvely, seeking to do the kind of character formation in fostering virtue that can be ultimately grounded rightly only in Christian faith. There are positive lessons to learn, nonetheless, from the endeavors of PP and how we understand human virtue and develop well-being.

---

[35] William Hurlbut, "Science, Ethics, and the Human Spirit," in *The Oxford Handbook of Religion and Science* (New York: Oxford University Press, 2008), 873.

✚ 6

PSYCHOLOGY OF RELIGION AND TRUTH

As an undergraduate psychology major in the 1970s, I took a course in the psychology of personality. At the end, I realized that though we had been through a rigorous consideration of many facets of personhood, not once in class or the readings had religion, spirituality, or morality been mentioned. This was the beginning of my understanding of the disconnection from, dismissal of, or hostility toward religion so common in this discipline.

Nevertheless, there has been among psychologists a stunning increase of interest in religion and spirituality. In this brief chapter, I will be drawing extensively from the magisterial handbook surveying the field of psychology of religion, published by the American Psychological Association.[1] Its editor documents this explosion of interest,[2] noting that there were 1,051 PsychINFO citations for the term *religion* in all of the 1960s but 11,629 in the 2000s (5 and 7,894, respectively, for the term *spirituality*).

One factor driving the surge of interest in religion and spirituality is that research points convincingly to the positive effects of religion. "Be it church attendance, belief in the afterlife, or religious commitment, traditional religious beliefs and practices in the United States appeared to have largely positive implications

---

[1] Kenneth I. Pargament, ed., *APA Handbook of Psychology, Religion, and Spirituality*, 2 vols. (Washington, DC: American Psychological Association, 2013).
[2] Kenneth I. Pargament, "Introduction," in *APA Handbook*, vol. 1, *xxiii*.

for health and well-being."[3] Another author offers a more detailed list of the benefits of religion and spirituality: "longer life; fewer depressive symptoms; higher levels of pro-social behavior; better marital functioning; less crime, delinquency, and drug use; higher school achievement; and even more frequent engagement in health behaviors, such as visiting the dentist, using seatbelts, and taking vitamins. These associations are robust and have been replicated with people from many religions and many nations."[4] On average, religion and spirituality appear to be good for people.

The psychology of religion and spirituality is not typically a topic covered in introductory psychology courses. But it is sometimes alluded to, and it is an area that may be of strong interest for faithful Christians. What are we to make of the scientific study of religion and spirituality? Can such psychological study inform the thoughtful Christian?

RELIGION AND SPIRITUALITY SEPARATED

The *APA Handbook* is structured around the presumption that religion and spirituality are distinguishable if interrelated aspects of human experience. This may be useful, as we will see in a moment, but it is important to emphasize yet again that our beliefs shape our perception of any phenomena that we study in science. I previously quoted Hood, who stated that "any [research] method is at least an implicit epistemology, and any epistemology assumes at least an implicit ontology. Simply put, how we seek to know assumes what we believe to be real."[5]

What psychologists presume as they approach the study of religious and spiritual matters shapes the subsequent scientific studies. It serves us well, then, to note how atypical psychologists are

[3] Kenneth I. Pargament, Annette Mahoney et al., "Envisioning an Integrative Paradigm for the Psychology of Religion and Spirituality," in *APA Handbook*, vol. 1, 13.
[4] Michael E. McCullough and Evan C. Carter, "Religion, Self-Control, and Self-Regulation: How Are They Related?," in *APA Handbook*, vol. 1, 123.
[5] Ralph W. Hood Jr., "Methodological Diversity in the Psychology of Religion and Spirituality," in *APA Handbook*, vol. 1, 79.

when it comes to religious faith. "In spite of cultural changes in the United States, . . . psychologists remain in many ways less R/S than other Americans."[6] In contrast to the general public, psychologists are (1) "substantially less likely to consider religion personally salient, with gaps ranging from 18% to 40%"; (2) "much more enthusiastic about spirituality" than about religion; (3) "more than six times more likely to have stopped believing in God at some point in the past"; and (4) disproportionately less likely to identify as Protestant or Catholic Christians, while the "proportion of Jewish respondents and members of other religions were consistently and substantially higher than in the national sample."[7]

Sometimes this reaction intensifies to antipathy, particularly toward religion. Pargament notes that the terms *religion* and *spirituality* have become "increasingly polarized from each other. In the 21st century, social scientists often form striking contrasts between the two terms: religion as institutional versus spirituality as individual, religion as external and objective versus spirituality as internal and subjective, religion as old versus spirituality as new, religion as structural versus spirituality as functional, religion as fixed and frozen versus spirituality as flexible and dynamic, and even religion as bad versus spirituality as good."[8] Pargament hints that the distinction between religion and spirituality may be fueled by antagonism toward religion.

Pargament defines *spirituality* as "the search for the sacred," and he defines *religion* as "the search for significance that occurs within the context of established institutions that are designed to facilitate spirituality."[9] This definition conceptualizes spirituality in a subjective fashion, emphasizing the search as an ongoing journey and the focus of that search as directed toward whatever the indi-

---

[6] Edward P. Shafranske and Jeremy P. Cummings, "Religious and Spiritual Beliefs, Affiliations, and Practices of Psychologists," in *APA Handbook*, vol. 2, 33.
[7] Ibid., 24–28.
[8] Ibid., 11.
[9] Ibid., 14–15.

vidual believes to be ultimate, transcendent, or divine. Religious institutions are construed broadly as systems of belief (doctrines, traditions, theologies, worldviews, and so forth) as well as sociological and cultural institutions (formalized practices, denominations, religious institutions, cultural traditions, and so forth).

Is this distinction between religion and spirituality legitimate and helpful? Certainly, Christians would have strident objections to the ridiculous formulation that religion is old, rigid, impersonal, and destructive, while spirituality is new, fluid, personal, and adaptive. But if we focus on Pargament's understanding of spirituality as the *individual search* for the sacred, and religion as those *structures* (including belief systems, traditions of practice, and human organizations) that are *designed to facilitate spirituality*, we may be inclined not to object.

This is especially the case when we realize that even though we are used to thinking of Christianity as a religion, the concept of religion is itself alien to the Bible. The term *Christianity* is not biblical. In the Scriptures, people are invited to follow Christ, to die to self and be born again, and to believe, be baptized, and be saved. Though certain nonbelievers called early believers "Christians" (Acts 11:26; 26:28), the believers themselves did not appear to use this term, instead referring to themselves as following or "belonging to the Way" (Acts 9:2; see also 19:9, 23; 22:4), indicating that their focus was on a journey or calling, much in accord with Pargament's emphasis on a spiritual journey.

But clearly it is also true that institutions emerged from the work of the early church. The very realities mentioned by Pargament—doctrines, traditions, theologies, worldviews, formalized practices, church buildings, monasteries, seminaries, denominations, and so forth—formed as a result of the work of the church. And as he describes, the purpose of all of these is "to facilitate spirituality," albeit spirituality of a distinctively Christian nature.

If the Christian faith is true, each of us is made for giving our lives to eternal realities. In this light, there is probably nothing intrinsically wrong with sorting the complexities of our human experience into the categories of religion and spirituality. At the same time, we may want to remember that our own human complexity and the infinite complexities of the supernatural transcend any of our categorizations. Just as the human complexities of a shy person are not captured or exhausted by the trite summarization, "Oh, she's just introverted," so also we must remember that the designations of "religion" and "spirituality" are helpful but limited categories.

We must be particularly resistant to the characterization that religion is necessarily old, rigid, impersonal, and destructive. Contemporary proponents of spirituality often presume that the supernatural, whatever it is, is passively waiting while human beings actively scramble (always partially) to understand it. But the Christian faith suggests something entirely different: that human beings are staggering around in the blindness of sin and that God reveals himself and his truth decisively, inviting us to embrace that truth.

If we believe that God reveals himself, then it is only proper that our spirituality conform itself to that revealed truth. Thus, true spirituality (our subjective search) should ultimately merge with religion (God's ordained revelation and the structures that have been formed upon it for the purpose of guiding us into a deeper walk with Christ). This confidence is tempered, though, by our understanding that our religious structures never perfectly mirror the God-revealed truth that inspired them.

IS RELIGION PRIMARY OR DERIVATIVE?

We consider next whether religion and spirituality are primary or derivative in human experience. Based on research showing the relative disinterest, nonengagement, and disbelief of psychologists, it is no surprise that many psychologists believe that religion is derivative, a curious and unnecessary by-product of other psychological and human processes. We are presumed to be religious, for instance, as a reaction to something more primary such as fear of death and nonexistence.

This intersects with one of the bigger themes of the field of psychology: the tendency to analyze human psychological phenomena by the functions the phenomena serve. The psychologist of religion who assumes religion and spirituality are derivative of something more fundamental asks, "What psychological function does religion serve for people?"[10] The second major section of the *APA Handbook* examines "Explanatory Models for Why People Are Religious and Spiritual." The first two major approaches share the striking commonality of emphasizing the role or function of religion in the management of anxiety.

DEFENSE AGAINST DEATH ANXIETY

"A primary function of religion is to buffer the individual against anxiety. . . . A core source of anxiety [is] the awareness that the self will inevitably die." This approach has been termed "terror management theory" and specifically proposes that "people manage the potential anxiety stemming from their awareness of mortality by subscribing to *cultural worldviews*, which afford opportunities to view life as valuable and continuing on in some way after death. From this perspective, religiousness serves to buffer anxiety about mortality by offering opportunities to attain immortality, thereby making death less threatening."[11] Historical figures such as William James and Sigmund Freud have promoted this theory, as have many subsequent theorists in psychoanalytic, existential, and other traditions.

In support, empirical studies have found correlations between measures of death anxiety and religious commitment, with higher religious commitment correlated with lower levels of death anxiety.

---

[10] Melissa Soenke, Mark J. Landau, and Jeff Greenberg, "Sacred Armor: Religion's Role as a Buffer against the Anxieties of Life and Fear of Death," in *APA Handbook*, vol. 1, 105.
[11] Ibid., emphasis original.

While most of this research has been conducted with Christian populations, similar results are emerging from studies of Muslim and other religious communities. Another type of supporting research finds that events that precipitate broad awareness of death (such as the 9/11 tragedy) are correlated with surges in church attendance, Bible sales, and visits to religious websites. "So, beneath all of religion's complexities, [fear of] death . . . keeps the appeal of religion very much alive."[12] In summary, religion and spirituality are derivative of the fear of death.

DIVINE ATTACHMENT

"An individual who has been fortunate in having grown up in an ordinary good home with ordinarily affectionate parents has always known people from whom he can seek support, comfort, and protection, and where they are to be found. So deeply established are his expectations and so repeatedly have they been confirmed that, as an adult, he finds it difficult to imagine any other kind of world."[13] In contrast to Sigmund Freud, who assumed that individuals with poor relationships with parents would be more likely to be religious, the attachment approach assumes that individuals with good attachment relationships to primary caregivers will generalize their positive expectations into the realm of religion and spirituality. A wide array of research has demonstrated striking similarities between one's perceptions of one's relationships to one's parents and one's perceived relationship to God or a divine figure. These researchers then believe that one's religion or spirituality is a projection outward of one's basic attachment strategies and needs.

Congruent with the prior approach, the attachment approach assumes "that religion provides surrogate attachment figures (most notably gods) that may be used to regulate the stress and gain a

---

[12] Ibid., 118.
[13] Attachment theorist John Bowlby, quoted in Pehr Granqvist and Lee A. Kirkpatrick, "Religion, Spirituality, and Attachment," in *APA Handbook*, vol. 1, 139.

sense of 'felt security.'"[14] This approach relies on research show-ing that young children with healthy parental attachment use the parent as a safe haven in times of stress or threat and a secure base from which to explore a potentially threatening world and expand their skills. In contrast, ambivalent or insecure attachment disrupts the child's sense of safety and complicates development. Attachment theorists tend to regard individuals with healthy at-tachment backgrounds as extending these healthy expectations to a relationship with the divine, while individuals with ambiguous or insecure attachment backgrounds experience ambivalence both in their human relationships and with the divine. Tellingly, the sum-mary of this approach argues that "no model of interpersonal rela-tionships in general, or attachment relationships in particular, will be complete without explicit acknowledgment of the role of God *and other imaginary figures* in people's relationship networks."[15] In summary, in this view religion and spirituality are derivative of our more primary attachment relations with parental figures.

The next two approaches are quite different, focusing on the role of religion and spirituality in fostering positive developmental outcomes for the individual and for groups.

SELF-CONTROL AND SELF-REGULATION

Research conclusively shows that religion and spirituality pro-duce positive health and adjustment outcomes. The self-control approach assumes that such outcomes are the primary function that is served by religion and spirituality, and therefore its perpetu-ation is a secondary by-product of these primary outcomes. "We hypothesize that religion fosters the development and exercise of self-control and self-regulation, which lead to beneficial outcomes in a variety of behavioral and psychological domains."[16] Drawing from the Darwinian concept of natural selection to explain religion

---

[14] Ibid.
[15] Ibid., 151, emphasis added.
[16] McCullough and Carter, "Religion, Self-Control, and Self-Regulation," 124.

and spirituality, these theorists invoke the concept of cultural selection, proposing that "many religious beliefs and behaviors take their contemporary forms in part because evolved psychological mechanisms for cultural learning and transmission cause people to acquire, modify, and retain and (perhaps) transmit those beliefs and behaviors to others in light of the beneficial consequences for self-control."[17]

The core evidence in support points to religious belief and institutions fostering the development of self-regulation and self-control, such as the evidence that religious families tend to have children with more self-control skills; further, "religious people tend to score higher on measures of self-control, and measures of personality that subsume self-control, such as conscientiousness and agreeableness, than do their less religious counterparts."[18] In summary, religion and spirituality persist as a derivative of their value in fostering self-control and self-regulation.

MOTIVATION FOR MEANING

This approach assumes "that a deeply rooted need for a functional meaning system underlies the highly prevalent embrace of religion across time and place. . . . [Religion and spirituality] is generally a highly functional way to satisfy the need for a meaning system. . . . This need is generally described as a drive to understand one's experience and to feel that one's life has significance and purpose,"[19] especially under conditions of stress or threat. Such a coherent system gives people a sense of mastery or control over their circumstances, both currently and in the future, and that sense of mastery and control helps them cope with the difficulties of living. These understandings also serve in the regulation of emotional response and assist in the maintenance of a sense

---

[17] Ibid.

[18] Ibid., 127.

[19] Crystal L. Park, Donald Edmondson, and Amy Hale-Smith, "Why Religion? Meaning as Motivation," in *APA Handbook*, vol. 1, 157.

of personal identity. Further, "humans require a system of goals (desired future states) to guide them in structuring their lives. A goal hierarchy, directing behavior from the most mundane to the most profound, is a core aspect of meaning systems. These goals are essential for providing an overarching purpose and direction to an individual's life."[20]

Evidence in support of this approach overlaps with much of that cited in support of prior theories, but it interprets that evidence as supporting the meaning-making function of religion, producing the positive ends produced by religious belief. In summary, religion and spirituality are derivative of the fundamental human need for meaning.

Should Christians object to the idea that religion helps us cope with the fear of death? That religion is driven by a desire for attachment to a secure parental figure? That religious faith "works" because it fosters self-control or a system of meaning? In chapter 3 we talked about reductionism, the tendency to collapse complex phenomena (the derivative phenomena) into simpler, more primary phenomena. I would argue that none of these proposed functions of religion are illicit but that none are primary; thus religion cannot be reduced to them. Briefly:

- Those without a living relationship with Christ *should* fear death. Christ repeatedly warns in the Gospels about the danger of being cast into hell (Matt. 5:29; 10:28; 18:9; Luke 12:5). This approach can mistakenly presume that death is nothing to be feared, but if the Bible is correct, we need salvation in Christ, just as the person facing a crouching tiger desperately needs rescue.

- We are made for relationships, first with God and then with people we love, and thus we have attachment capacities. In Christian perspective, far from good parenting leading to a fantasy relationship with an illusory God, God himself instructs in Deuteronomy 6:1–9 that parents are to deliberately structure their parenting and home

---

[20] Ibid., 159.

life to direct the child's experience toward a loving expectation of future relationship with God, the Father of all.

- The proper progression of growth in Christ is toward self-control, which is listed as one of the fruits of the Spirit (Gal. 5:23) and one of the strengths or virtues we are to pursue (2 Pet. 1:5). The book of Proverbs and other Wisdom Literature of the Old Testament testify that God commends the development of self-control and self-regulation as avenues to blessing and prosperity. These virtues should have positive results in our lives. Virtue is not the cause of religion and spirituality but the result of it.

- The Bible makes clear that sincere pursuit of life in Christ gives one a sense of meaning. When many of the superficial followers of Christ turned away from him, the twelve apostles stuck with him because, as Peter testified, "Lord, to whom shall we go? You have the words of eternal life" (John 6:68). They had properly come to find it inconceivable that they could understand life apart from the perspective that Christ gave to them.

There is nothing illegitimate about any of these functions that religion is presumed to serve. We must disagree, however, with the argument that any of these meanings—individually or in combination—are primary and religious faith thus derivative. Yes, religion and spirituality serve these functions. A nonbeliever may speculate that religion persists only because of the functions, but believers would contend otherwise. It is not just Christians who respond this way; the *Handbook's* editor, Kenneth Pargament, a devout Jew, observes:

Traditionally, theorists in the social sciences have assumed that religious beliefs and practices are expressions of [i.e., derivative from] something presumably more basic, be it the need for emotional comfort, relief from the terror of dying, control of human impulses, social connectedness, evolutionary advantage, or meaning and purpose. . . . Although these explanations clarify the workings of religion and spirituality, they overlook a simpler possibility—that spirituality reflects a distinctive, in some ways irreducible [i.e., primary] human motivation, a yearning for the sacred.[21]

Our understanding of creation suggests that religiousness and spirituality are *primary* phenomena. In Christian understanding, human beings are made for worship, made for relationship with God. The first pair of the Ten Commandments—that we shall have no other gods beside the true God and shall not worship idols—suggests that perhaps our most fundamental characteristic is that we will worship something. It is not an understatement to say that to be a *homo sapien* is to be a *homo religio*. We will worship something, but what will we worship?

Finally and too superficially, we should note one of the greatest perplexities for Christians related to this argument: the positive results generated by religion and spirituality have been shown to be roughly equivalent across multiple religions. Doesn't this indicate that it doesn't much matter what you believe, as long as you believe something? This profound question deserves a longer answer, but the best summary response is to point out that (a) if we are made to be religious beings, then counterfeit religious faith is probably better than no religious faith at all and will serve some of the same functions; (b) God's adversary, the Devil, no doubt seeks to draw people away from true faith by generating some types of positive results through other faiths; and (c) as Christians, we believe in the primary authority of God's Word and the exclusive claims of Jesus Christ so that we must affirm that the *content* of our belief matters.

FACTORS THAT SHAPE RELIGIOUS EXPERIENCE

There is quite a bit of additional research on factors that shape or moderate the experience of religion and spirituality. I briefly summarize here some of the most interesting:

---

[21] Kenneth I. Pargament, "Searching for the Sacred: Toward a Nonreductionistic Theory of Spirituality," in *APA Handbook*, vol. 1, 257.

Neurophysiology. A substantive body of research has examined the intriguing question of what happens in the brain when people have religious experiences. The research has focused on two different sets of phenomena: extraordinary/mystical (ecstatic) experience, and more commonplace religious practices (such as prayer or meditation).[22]

This approach gained its earliest impetus from clinical observations of patients with temporal lobe epilepsy, a good number of whom experience mystical experiences at the time of seizures. This has led some neurological reductionists to dismiss religious experience as a function of a disordered brain and even to search for a "god module" in the brain. Thankfully, these have been the exception; increasingly, researchers attempt to understand how various parts of the brain moderate, process, and structure religious experience.

The findings suggest that mystical or ecstatic experiences tend to involve those parts of the brain most deeply connected to emotion, namely, the temporal lobes and the limbic system. More common religious practices tend to be associated with activation of the frontal and parietal cortex areas, those areas associated with the development of self-control and self-regulation, though with some activation of the limbic system. Interestingly, some studies of the charismatic practice of glossolalia (speaking in tongues, which some might presume to be primarily an emotional experience) have demonstrated its association with the activation of the frontal and parietal cortex areas.

Should the Christian find troubling the association of religious experience with specific parts of the brain? Not at all. The fact that we are embodied beings, and specifically neurologically grounded beings (chapter 3), should lead us to expect that religious experiences—as *real* experiences—will be manifested in neurological events.

---

[22] Joanna Maselko, "The Neurophysiology of Religious Experience," in *APA Handbook*, vol. 1.

Cognitive science (CS). Neuroscience looks at how the brain functions physiologically; CS looks at how the human brain/mind processes information according to its own functional rules and processes. The relationship of neuroscience and CS might be analogous to the levels at which a computer processes information: the electrical and physical engineering properties of the computing system are a fundamental material reality (analogous to human neurophysiology), and on top of that are built different levels of programming languages. CS attempts to understand mental functioning at such a higher-order level.

The CS approach sees religion as built into the way that the brain processes information. These patterns determine the shape and texture of how information is interpreted in relationship to the transcendent. This approach has generated interesting findings about the propensity of children to believe in the supernatural, in causation, and in meaning.[23] Researchers have found, for instance, that children are strongly prone to believe in the afterlife and to exhibit *"promiscuous teleology*: a tendency to find design and purpose in the natural world"[24] (i.e., children often understand impersonal events as occurring for personal, intentional purposes, as in, "It rained because God wanted to water the grass"). There is research suggesting the children are disposed to believe in a (or many) divine agent(s) possessing superhuman knowledge, power, and immortality. These results suggest that children are "born believers."[25]

This in turn leads to an interesting possible reinterpretation of a commonly reported correlation. Some research suggests that as education and intelligence increase, religious dedication and fervor tend to decrease. The typical secular interpretation is that

---

[23] Justin L. Barrett and Bonnie Poon Zahl, "Cognition, Evolution, and Religion," in *APA Handbook*, vol. 1.

[24] Ibid., 225, emphasis original.

[25] Justin Barrett, *Born Believers: The Science of Children's Religious Belief* (New York: Free Press, 2012).

ignorance fosters religious faith, so as education increases, religion decreases. The alternative possibility is that religious faithfulness is the natural state of humanity but that Western educators, biased against traditional religion and spirituality, suppress these natural impulses in children, with the result that as education increases, religion and spirituality decrease.

Should Christians be concerned about CS approaches to religion and spirituality? No. Humans were made for relationship with God; it makes perfect sense that the standard patterns by which our minds process information would point toward rather than away from faith in God.

The religious personality trait. This approach argues conceptually and empirically for religion and spirituality as a fundamental dimension of human personality. We discussed previously the "Big 5" trait theory of personality; this approach argues that there is a *sixth* big trait necessary to round out our understanding of human personality: the religion and spirituality trait.[26] Measures of religion and spirituality are consistently only moderately correlated with the other Big 5 traits, suggesting that religion and spirituality are fundamentally different from and independent of the other major dimensions of personality. Though some might argue that religion and spirituality are merely a type of life outcome from the interaction of the other Big 5 traits (i.e., derivative of other traits of personality), proponents of this approach argue that religion and spirituality are more basic and fundamental traits. Empirical exploration into the measurement of religion and spirituality has suggested a number of possible dimensions of religious experience, but this research is in its earliest stages.

Once again, Christians have no particular reason to quarrel with the possibility that religiousness is a fundamental trait of human personality. This finding does pose complications for what

---

[26] Ralph Piedmont and Teresa A. Wilkins, "Spirituality, Religiousness, and Personality: Theoretical Foundations and Empirical Applications," in *APA Handbook*, vol 1.

we are to make of the religious culpability of the person who is naturally disinclined toward religious faith, but we have no guarantee that life is perfectly equitable. Each of us is born with traits that incline us in positive directions and others that incline us in negative directions. Our responsibility is to make good choices in the context of these inclinations.

PSYCHOLOGY OF RELIGION AND TRUTH

There is much, much more that we could explore in the psychology of religion. The *APA Handbook* does an extraordinary job of presenting the breadth and complexity of this subfield, including such matters as:

- issues of methodology in studying religion and spirituality and the many complexities and problems in measuring religion and spirituality;

- studies of various types of religious and spiritual expression and experience such as prayer, meditation, ritual, religious coping, mystical experience, religion and altruism, and spiritual struggles;

- religion and spirituality across a variety of populations, from children to the elderly, from the extremely devout to agnostics and apostates, and across religious traditions and ethnic groups; and

- the newer and growing field of applied psychology of religion and spirituality, covering such topics as religion and spirituality from the perspective of major approaches to human change such as psychodynamic, cognitive, and family systems.

We close, however, by asking the most fundamental question: Is the object (or objects) toward which religious and spiritual sentiment is directed *real*? Is human religion and spirituality a response to a clearly revealed reality, a tentative response to existential ambiguity, or a delusional response to illusion? Such a question is beyond the capacity of science to answer, but some grappling with this issue help us to get our bearings as we think about the psychology of religion and spirituality.

As we have already discussed, some secular psychologists would argue that because religion and spirituality serve certain psychological functions, it therefore exists *because of* these functions—*derivative to* these functions—and not because those functions point to transcendent realities. Such assertions can undermine our belief in the truth of religious faith.

But this danger is based on a logical error. Friends serve a need for relationship, and a spouse serves a need for deeper relationship and sexual intimacy, but despite serving these needs, friends and spouses really do exist! If God exists and made human beings with the capacity to know him, isn't it logical that we would find ourselves tuned to detect his existence, inclined to be religious and spiritual, and designed to be on a spiritual journey? Such logic was a staple of C. S. Lewis's defense of Christianity:

> A man's physical hunger does not prove that a man will get any bread; he may die of starvation on a raft in the Atlantic. But surely a man's hunger does prove that he comes from a race which repairs its body by eating and inhabits a world where eatable substances exist. In the same way, though I do not believe (I wish I did) that my desire for Paradise proves that I shall enjoy it, I think it a pretty good indication that such a thing exists and that some men will.[27]

Of course, this argument is not philosophically watertight, and creative counterarguments are possible. Freud's view of religion as father-projection to ward off anxiety works *when* the assumption is made that God does not exist. But such a flexible speculation can be turned on itself. When we start with the contrasting presumption that God does exist, we then can conclude that atheism is the result of father-rejection.

---

[27] C. S. Lewis, "The Weight of Glory," in *Transposition: And Other Addresses* (London: Geoffrey Bles, 1949), 23.

We can extrapolate to other dimensions of this question of the reality of the transcendent. First, we may note that just as hungry man's desire for bread is some indication that bread really exists, so also it is possible that the buffering effect of religion and spirituality with regard to anxiety over death does not indicate that religion is a helpful delusion. Instead, it may indicate that death is real and really is something to be feared, and that God designed us to embrace a defense against death in the form of faith in Jesus Christ.

Second, the positive benefits, on average, of religion and spirituality provide at least some support for the notion that humans were designed for a relationship with the divine. Complex evolutionary, psychoanalytic, and other arguments for how such beliefs and practices could be productive, even though they are delusions, are credible in some ways. But the sheer weight of the evidence that religion and spirituality have a positive impact upon human functioning points toward religion and spirituality being human responses to something real.

In conclusion, the human reality is that Christians are in the same position as psychologists of religion and spirituality: it is our human responsibility to try to make sense of the cacophony of claims about religious faith in the world. The psychology of religion and spirituality can be of assistance to thoughtful Christians in making sense of this cacophony, but only if we keep firmly in mind the Christian convictions that:

- the distinction between religion and spirituality is a helpful, pragmatic distinction, but the grand reality of God's work in the world through Christ exhausts and supersedes these human categories;

- religion and spirituality at times can be derivative of or secondary to other psychological processes (such as when an epileptic has a mystical experience as part of a seizure), but generally speaking, religion and spirituality are fundamental and primary human characteristics because we are made to worship the one true God; and

- the ways in which religion and spirituality serve psychological and other purposes—far from undermining the reality of the transcendent—serve to strengthen our conviction that the supernatural is real and demands our response.

QUESTIONS FOR REFLECTION

1) The Enlightenment mind-set seeks objective, indisputable, universal knowledge; postmodernists argue that truth is always relative, constructed, and subjective. How can Christians acknowledge the constraints on what we can know and still have a meaningful understanding of truth and our human capacity to know it?

2) What are the most important elements of what it means to be made in the image of God? How does our biological embodiedness (including the structures of our brains and the influences of our genes) shape this reality?

3) What evidence do you find to be the most supportive of the idea that higher human capacities (mind, soul, spirit) emerge from and transcend our embodiment? What evidence do you find that most substantially challenges this idea?

4) If a new empirical study found that the propensity toward prayer had a strong genetic heritability of 0.60, how would that influence the likelihood that you would adopt a new discipline of prayer? Should it, and why?

5) Which virtues and character strengths do you believe to be most similar across two different religious traditions with which you are familiar, and which differ the most profoundly and why?

6) Which of the four major approaches to explaining the function of religious belief best describes your own inclination toward your religious beliefs? How does reflection on this influence the certainty of your commitments?

GLOSSARY

Agent, Agency. When human beings (or supernatural beings) are construed as being able to rise above the causal forces shaping and constraining their behavior and to act in ways demonstrating some type of freedom (and hence meriting moral culpability), they are said to be acting as an agent or demonstrating agency.

Determinism. The claim that current human behavior is caused comprehensively by prior conditions, whether biological or environmental, thus leaving no room for meaningful human freedom. If determinism is true, then human beings are not agents.

Dualism. The claim that humans are constituted of two (dual) distinct types of essence: physical bodies and nonphysical minds/souls/spirits.

Emergentism. The claim that higher-order entities can arise or emerge from complex lower-order systems in such a way that the new higher-order system operates by rules different from and not reducible to the rules of the lower-order system from which it sprung; the human mind is said to emerge from and not be reduced to the physical brain.

Enlightenment. The intellectual movement from the sixteenth and seventeenth centuries that emphasized the primacy of human reason, rejected religious tradition as a source of knowledge, and embraced scientific methodologies as the most reliable source of truth.

Environmentalism. The dominant or exclusive emphasis on one's material and social environment as the source of causal influences on current behavior.

Epistemology. One's theory of knowledge; one's approach to the pursuit of truth.

Heritability. A statistical estimate ranging from 0.00 to 1.00 of the proportion of the variation in a given measurement of behavior or personality that can be attributed to genetic influences.

Monism. The philosophical commitment that there is only one (mono) type of essence that forms human beings; most monists believe we are completely physical beings and that there are no nonphysical aspects of persons.

Monozygotic twins. Mono (one) zygote (egg) twins; twins that exist because a fertilized egg split into two separate fetuses within hours or days of conception, resulting in what are informally called identical twins.

Ontology. One's theory of existence of what is real; what one assumes to be the basic nature of reality.

Original sin. The traditional Christian teaching, usually attributed to Augustine, that the taint of sin is universal in the human race and passed across the generations at conception.

Postmodernism. Post (after) modernism (the Enlightenment mind-set is also called "modernism"; hence postmodernism); the movement in reaction to the failures of the Enlightenment, which in its most radical forms denies our capacity to know truth (or even that truth exists) and emphasizes narrative and the primacy of individual experience.

Reductionism. The view that complex phenomena can be exhaustively explained in terms of simpler and more basic phenomena; often detected by use of the phrase "nothing but," as in, "Human emotion is nothing but neurons firing."

Spirituality and religion. Spirituality is the subjective search for or ongoing journey toward whatever the individual believes to be ultimate, transcendent, or divine; religion refers to systems of belief (doctrines, theologies, and so forth) as well as to institutions (practices, denominations, schools, and so forth) that structure spiritual experience.

Thomism; Thomistic theology. An approach to theology shaped by Thomas Aquinas (the term "Thomistic" comes from his first name) in which the philosophy of Aristotle is used to extend and adapt Christian theological exploration.

Total depravity. The traditional Christian teaching, emphasized in Calvinistic theology, that every aspect of human experience is tainted and touched by sin; the most frequent counter-foil to total depravity is the Thomistic suggestion that human will is profoundly corrupted by sin, but that human reason is largely unaffected.

RESOURCES FOR FURTHER STUDY

CHAPTERS 1 AND 2

Beck, James, and Bruce Demarest, *The Human Person in Theology and Psychology: A Biblical Anthropology for the 21st Century*. Grand Rapids, MI: Kregel, 2005.

A useful overview of theological anthropology as it relates to psychology.

Brooke, John H. *Science and Religion*. Cambridge, UK: Cambridge University Press, 1991.

A classic volume demonstrating responsible reflection on the relationship between science and Christianity.

Davis, Jeffrey C., and Philip G. Ryken. *Liberal Arts for the Christian Life*. Wheaton, IL: Crossway, 2012.

Covers a wide array of issues in the Christian intellectual life.

Dockery, David, and Timothy George. *The Great Tradition of Christian Thinking: A Student's Guide*. Reclaiming the Christian Intellectual Tradition. Wheaton, IL: Crossway, 2012.

Johnson, Eric L., ed. *Psychology and Christianity: Five Views*. 2nd edition. Downers Grove, IL: InterVarsity, 2010.

A good, general introduction to the relationship of psychology and Christianity. Johnson's chapter, "A Brief History of Christians in Psychology" (pp. 9–47), is a magisterial summary of how Christians have engaged psychological topics through history. My chapter, "An Integration View," is an extended presentation of my argument for how to relate Christian faith to psychology.

Jones, Stanton L., and Richard Butman. *Modern Psychotherapies: A Comprehensive Christian Appraisal*. 2nd edition. Downers Grove, IL: InterVarsity, 2011.

Noll, Mark. *Jesus Christ and the Life of the Mind*. Grand Rapids, MI: Eerdmans, 2011.

An inspiring call to Christ-centered intellectual life by one of the greatest Christian intellectuals writing today.

Ryken, Philip G. *Christian Worldview: A Student's Guide*. Recovering the Christian Intellectual Tradition. Wheaton, IL: Crossway, 2013.

Yarhouse, Mark A., Richard E. Butman, and Barrett W. McRay. *Modern Psychopathologies: A Comprehensive Christian Appraisal*. Downers Grove, IL: InterVarsity, 2005.

Helpful general overviews of issues involved in relating Christian views of the person and personality to counseling theory and method, psychopathology, and related issues.

CHAPTER 3

Struthers, William M. *Wired for Intimacy: How Pornography Hijacks the Male Brain.* Downers Grove, IL: InterVarsity, 2009.

>   Struthers overviews a great deal of information about brain functioning in discussing sexuality and sexual addiction in Christian perspective.

CHAPTER 4

Jones, Stanton L., and Richard Butman, *Modern Psychotherapies: A Comprehensive Christian Appraisal.* 2nd edition. Downers Grove, IL: InterVarsity, 2011.

>   Contains helpful extended summaries and Christian reflections on the major personality theories.

Segal, Nancy L. *Born Together—Reared Apart: The Landmark Minnesota Twins Study.* Cambridge, MA: Harvard University Press, 2012.

>   A readable overview of MISTRA.

CHAPTER 5

Jones, Stanton L., and Richard Butman, *Modern Psychotherapies: A Comprehensive Christian Appraisal.* 2nd edition. Downers Grove, IL: InterVarsity, 2011.

Yarhouse, Mark A., Richard E. Butman, and Barrett W. McRay, *Modern Psychopathologies: A Comprehensive Christian Appraisal.* Downers Grove, IL: InterVarsity, 2005.

CHAPTER 6

Barrett, Justin. *Born Believers: The Science of Children's Religious Belief* (New York: Free Press, 2012).

>   An intriguing application of cognitive science to religious belief by a psychologist at Fuller Theological Seminary.

Paloutzian, Raymond F. *Invitation to the Psychology of Religion,* 2nd edition. Boston: Allyn & Bacon, 1996.

>   A classic volume, perhaps available by interlibrary loan, that is an accessible introduction to the psychology of religion.

GENERAL INDEX

✚ CHECK OUT THE OTHER BOOKS IN THE
**RECLAIMING THE CHRISTIAN
INTELLECTUAL TRADITION SERIES**

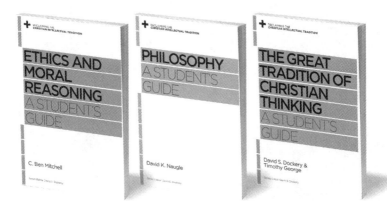

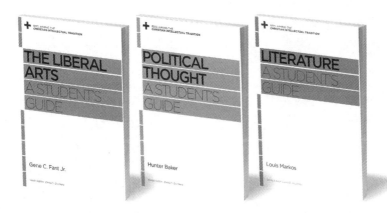

For more information, visit crossway.org.